EFFECTIVE DIGITAL LEARNING ENVIRONMENTS

Your Guide to the ISTE Standards
FOR COACHES

Jo Williamson

International Society for Technology in Education
EUGENE, OREGON • ARLINGTON, VA

Effective Digital Learning Environments
Your Guide to the ISTE Standards for Coaches
Jo Williamson

Editor: Emily Reed
Production Manager: Christine Longmuir
Copy Editor: Kathleen Hamman
Book Design and Production: Jeff Puda

Library of Congress Cataloging-in-Publication Data

Names: Williamson, Jo (Jo E.) author.
Title: Effective digital learning environments : your guide to the ISTE
   standards for coaches / Jo Williamson.
Description: First Edition. | Eugene, Oregon : International Society for
   Technology in Education, 2015.
Identifiers: LCCN 2015031664 | ISBN 9781564843678 (paperback)
Subjects: LCSH: Educational technology–Standards. | Educational
   technology–Planning. | International Society for Technology in Education.
   | BISAC: EDUCATION / Computers & Technology. | EDUCATION / Teaching
   Methods & Materials / General.
Classification: LCC LB1028.3 .W553 2015 | DDC 371.33–dc23
LC record available at http://lccn.loc.gov/2015031664

First Edition
ISBN: 978-1-56484-367-8
Ebook version available.

Printed in the United States of America

ISTE® is a registered trademark of the International Society for Technology in Education.

About ISTE

The International Society for Technology in Education (ISTE) is the premier nonprofit organization serving educators and education leaders committed to empowering connected learners in a connected world. ISTE serves more than 100,000 education stakeholders throughout the world.

ISTE's innovative offerings include the ISTE Conference & Expo, one of the biggest, most comprehensive ed tech events in the world—as well as the widely adopted ISTE Standards for learning, teaching, and leading in the digital age and a robust suite of professional learning resources, including webinars, online courses, consulting services for schools and districts, books, and peer-reviewed journals and publications. Visit iste.org to learn more.

ALSO BY JO WILLIAMSON

ISTE's Technology Facilitation and Leadership Standards

RELATED ISTE TITLES

Making Technology Standards Work for You, Susan Brooks-Young

A Constructivist Approach to the National Educational Technology Standards for Teachers,
V.N. Morphew

About the Author

Jo Williamson, Ph.D is associate professor in the Instructional Technology Department at Kennesaw State University, Kennesaw, Georgia. In this role, she focuses on training future technology coaches for K–12 schools. She serves as a course designer, instructor, and program coordinator for fully online graduate programs built on the ISTE Standards for Technology Coaches (ISTE Standards • C). Prior to joining the KSU faculty in 2005, Williamson served as director of Educational Technology & Media for the Georgia Department of Education; the director of Area One Technology Hub for the Illinois State Department of Education; and director of Technology for Waukegan, Illinois, Public Schools. She holds a bachelor's degree in English education from Olivet Nazarene University, Bourbonnais, Illinois; a master's degree in curriculum and instruction from the University of Kansas, Lawrence; and a doctorate in curriculum and instruction from the University of Illinois, Urbana-Champaign.

Contents

Preface and Acknowledgments

Released in 2011, the ISTE Standards for Technology Coaches (ISTE Standards•C) are the newest ISTE standards. They join ISTE Standards for Students (ISTE Standards•S, 2007); ISTE Standards for Teachers (ISTE Standards•T, 2008); and ISTE Standards for Administrators (ISTE Standards•A, 2009).

The ISTE Standards•C are important because technology coaches are important. Without technology coaches, we are unlikely to see the full implementation of other ISTE standards. The ISTE Standards•C describe how technology coaches provide critical contributions in the following categories:

- Visionary Leadership

- Teaching, Learning, and Assessment

- Digital Age Learning Environments

- Professional Development and Program Evaluation

- Digital Citizenship

- Content Knowledge and Professional Growth

This book provides an in-depth look at the ISTE Standards for Technology Coaches and illuminates the critical roles they play in transforming schools into digital age learning environments.

The ISTE Standards•C were created with extensive input from technology coaches practicing in K–12 schools. The final draft was created by ISTE's Accreditation and Standards Committee. This committee included the following members:

Sheryl R. Abshire, Calcasieu Parish Public Schools

David Barr, Administrator Emeritus, Illinois Mathematics and Science Academy

Arlene Borthwick, National Louis University

Kathy Hayden, California State University San Marcos

Peggy Kelly, California State Polytechnic University

Kay Lehman, Online Educator/Author

Anita McAnear, ISTE

Steve Rainwater, University of Texas at Tyler

Traci Redish, Kennesaw State University

Meg Swecker, Roanoke County Public Schools

Carolyn Sykora, ISTE

Lajeane Thomas (retired), Louisiana Tech University

Jo Williamson, Kennesaw State University

We hope this book will help recognize and reinforce the role of technology coaches around the world!

—Brian Lewis
CEO, International Society for Technology in Education

Introduction

This book is designed to introduce you to the International Society for Technology in Education (ISTE) Standards for Technology Coaches (ISTE Standards • C) and to help you use them to advance the effective use of technology in your organization.

ISTE strategically chose the term "technology coach" to highlight the individualized, job-embedded professional learning teachers need to adopt and use technology in schools. Technology coaching is responsive, supportive, and differentiated, accommodating teachers' unique learning needs, styles, and preferences. Excellent technology coaches take responsibility for developing productive relationships with learners, ensuring that all types of educators experience success.

This Introduction will answer the following critical questions:

- Who are technology coaches?

- What are the ISTE Standards • C?

- How do the ISTE Standards • C relate to other ISTE standards for students, teachers, and administrators, including technology directors?

- How do the ISTE Standards • C relate to ISTE Essential Conditions?

- Why are the ISTE Standards • C important?

- Who should know about the ISTE Standards • C?

- How can I learn more about the ISTE Standards • C?

If you are exploring this book, you are probably interested in advancing technology use in schools. This makes you a practicing or aspiring technology coach!

Technology coaches are broadly defined as *educators who help others use technology effectively to improve teaching and learning.* These individuals and their activities, often unseen and underestimated, are key agents of positive change. Technology coaches guide colleagues through the transformation of traditional schools into digital age learning environments.

Some educators have full-time or part-time paid positions dedicated to technology coaching. Various school districts assign these employees a wide variety of titles, including technology coaches, technology integration specialists, technology facilitators, technology lead teachers, instructional designers, technology coordinators, or information and communication technology (ICT) integrators. School library media specialists most often serve as technology coaches, too.

In other cases, technology coaches may not have "technology" in their title. They may not even have technology coaching in their job descriptions. Yet, these educators find ways to integrate aspects of technology coaching into their daily routines or beyond-school activities. For example, teachers who experiment with technology in their own classrooms frequently help their colleagues incorporate tech into their teaching styles and clerical routines. Content area coordinators, literacy coaches, and instructional lead teachers frequently engage in technology coaching as part of their work. Principals and district technology directors often find themselves serving as technology coaches in addition to performing their administrative duties.

Most technology coaches are employed by school districts, but some technology coaches are self-employed or employed by for-profit companies, not-for-profit organizations, state departments of education, regional consortia, and university outreach programs. These coaches serve as external consultants to schools and districts on an as-needed basis.

To help you better understand the scope of technology coaching, this book contains 17 real-life case studies of coaches from across the United States and around the world. The coaches highlighted in the cases studies assume varied roles in their organizations; their stories illustrate many different ways of fulfilling the ISTE Standards•C.

What Are the ISTE Standards for Technology Coaches (ISTE Standards•C)?

Published by The International Society for Technology in Education (ISTE), the ISTE Standards•C describe what exemplary technology coaches should know and be able to do to help transform traditional, teacher-centered schools into effective digital age learning environments.

The ISTE Standards•C comprise six overarching standards and 28 elements. A full implementation of these standards and performance indicators is critical to supporting technology implementation in schools. How many standards individual coaches can address depends on how much time they can dedicate to helping others and the size of the population being served. Some coaches may find themselves working mainly within the areas described by one or two standards, while other coaches may find that they regularly need to implement all six standards.

The ISTE Standards • C are accompanied by the ISTE Technology Coaching Rubric (containing six categories) that describes performances at the *approaches, meets,* and *exceeds* levels. Of course, technology coaches should aspire to engage all the people they mentor at the highest levels possible, but various individuals' performances will depend on many factors, including knowledge, skills, experience, and system support for coaching activities.

This book will help you as a technology coach to understand the standards and adapt them to your school's or organization's unique setting. One chapter is dedicated to each of the six standards. These chapters also include in-depth examinations of the supporting elements, the ISTE Standards • C rubric, and other learning resources related to each standard.

ISTE Standards for Coaches (Standards•C)

1. VISIONARY LEADERSHIP

Technology coaches inspire and participate in the development and implementation of a shared vision for the comprehensive integration of technology to promote excellence and support transformational change throughout the instructional environment.

   a. Contribute to the development, communication and implementation of a shared vision for the comprehensive use of technology to support a digital age education for all students.

   b. Contribute to the planning, development, communication, implementation and evaluation of technology-infused strategic plans at the district and school levels.

   c. Advocate for policies, procedures, programs and funding strategies to support implementation of the shared vision represented in the school and district technology plans and guidelines.

   d. Implement strategies for initiating and sustaining technology innovations and manage the change process in schools and classrooms.

2. TEACHING, LEARNING AND ASSESSMENTS

Technology coaches assist teachers in using technology effectively for assessing student learning, differentiating instruction and providing rigorous, relevant and engaging learning experiences for all students.

   a. Coach teachers in and model design and implementation of technology-enhanced learning experiences addressing content standards and student technology standards.

   b. Coach teachers in and model design and implementation of technology-enhanced learning experiences using a variety of research-based, learner-centered instructional strategies and assessment tools to address the diverse needs and interests of all students.

   c. Coach teachers in and model engagement of students in local and global interdisciplinary units in which technology helps students assume professional roles, research real-world problems, collaborate with others and produce products that are meaningful and useful to a wide audience.

d. Coach teachers in and model design and implementation of technology-enhanced learning experiences emphasizing creativity, higher-order thinking skills and processes and mental habits of mind (e.g., critical thinking, meta-cognition and self-regulation).

e. Coach teachers in and model design and implementation of technology-enhanced learning experiences using differentiation, including adjusting content, process, product and learning environment based upon student readiness levels, learning styles, interests and personal goals.

f. Coach teachers in and model incorporation of research-based best practices in instructional design when planning technology-enhanced learning experiences.

g. Coach teachers in and model effective use of technology tools and resources to continuously assess student learning and technology literacy by applying a rich variety of formative and summative assessments aligned with content and student technology standards.

h. Coach teachers in and model effective use of technology tools and resources to systematically collect and analyze student achievement data, interpret results and communicate findings to improve instructional practice and maximize student learning.

3. DIGITAL AGE LEARNING ENVIRONMENTS

Technology coaches create and support effective digital age learning environments to maximize the learning of all students.

a. Model effective classroom management and collaborative learning strategies to maximize teacher and student use of digital tools and resources and access to technology-rich learning environments.

b. Maintain and manage a variety of digital tools and resources for teacher and student use in technology-rich learning environments.

c. Coach teachers in and model use of online and blended learning, digital content and collaborative learning networks to support and extend student learning as well as expand opportunities and choices for online professional development for teachers and administrators.

d. Select, evaluate and facilitate the use of adaptive and assistive technologies to support student learning.

e. Troubleshoot basic software, hardware and connectivity problems common in digital learning environments.

f. Collaborate with teachers and administrators to select and evaluate digital tools and resources that enhance teaching and learning and are compatible with the school technology infrastructure.

g. Use digital communication and collaboration tools to communicate locally and globally with students, parents, peers and the larger community.

4. PROFESSIONAL DEVELOPMENT AND PROGRAM EVALUATION

Technology coaches conduct needs assessments, develop technology-related professional learning programs and evaluate the impact on instructional practice and student learning.

   a. Conduct needs assessments to inform the content and delivery of technology-related professional learning programs that result in a positive impact on student learning.

   b. Design, develop and implement technology-rich professional learning programs that model principles of adult learning and promote digital age best practices in teaching, learning and assessment.

   c. Evaluate results of professional learning programs to determine the effectiveness on deepening teacher content knowledge, improving teacher pedagogical skills and/or increasing student learning.

5. DIGITAL CITIZENSHIP

Technology coaches model and promote digital citizenship.

   a. Model and promote strategies for achieving equitable access to digital tools and resources and technology-related best practices for all students and teachers.

   b. Model and facilitate safe, healthy, legal and ethical uses of digital information and technologies.

   c. Model and promote diversity, cultural understanding and global awareness by using digital age communication and collaboration tools to interact locally and globally with students, peers, parents and the larger community.

6. CONTENT KNOWLEDGE AND PROFESSIONAL GROWTH

Technology coaches demonstrate professional knowledge, skills and dispositions in content, pedagogical and technological areas as well as adult learning and leadership and are continuously deepening their knowledge and expertise.

   a. Engage in continual learning to deepen content and pedagogical knowledge in technology integration and current and emerging technologies necessary to effectively implement the ISTE Standards•S and ISTE Standards•T.

   b. Engage in continuous learning to deepen professional knowledge, skills and dispositions in organizational change and leadership, project management and adult learning to improve professional practice.

   c. Regularly evaluate and reflect on their professional practice and dispositions to improve and strengthen their ability to effectively model and facilitate technology-enhanced learning experiences.

Using the ISTE Standards•C and the ISTE Technology Coaching Rubric

The ISTE Standards • C are accompanied by an ISTE Standards • C Technology Coaching Rubric. This rubric can be used in many ways.

- Practicing and aspiring technology coaches can use the ISTE Standards • C rubric to reflect on their professional practices. Through their reflections, they can identify areas of strength and set goals for improvement.

- Those who supervise technology coaches can adapt the rubric to evaluate potential hires and perform annual reviews for practicing technology coaches.

- Since the Council for the Accreditation of Educational Programs (CAEP) has approved the rubric, university faculty can use the rubric to design graduate-level degree and certificate programs aligned with the ISTE Standards • C. During the accreditation process, CAEP reviewers will use the rubric to evaluate the quality of these programs.

Understanding the structure and logic of the rubric will help you maximize its use and understand references to the rubric in Chapters One through Six.

STRUCTURE OF THE ISTE STANDARDS•C RUBRIC

For each standard, the rubric describes three main levels of performance: (1) Approaches, (2) Meets, and (3) Exceeds. Several descriptive sentences follow each of the three levels. These descriptors clarify the knowledge and skills that individuals must demonstrate in order to attain each level of performance.

Approaches Level

Most performances at the Approaches Level describe the acquisition of foundational knowledge that technology coaches must have attained in order to enact the ISTE Standards • C. For the most part, these performances represent lower-level cognitive tasks such as remembering and understanding, with only a few requirements to analyze or apply. In the Approaches Level, technology coaches most often identify, define, and explain terms, principles, policies, issues, theories, strategies, tools, and best practices related to good technology coaching.

The following are examples of Approaches Level performances:

- Define the term "shared vision" and explain the importance of developing, communicating, and implementing a shared vision for technology use in schools and strategic plans to reach the vision (ISTE Standards • C, 2a).

- Identify technology literacy standards for students (ISTE Standards • S) and any local/state student technology standards that must be addressed in classroom instruction and develop strategies for integrating technology into content-area instruction. (ISTE Standards • C, 2a)

At the Approaches Level, a few performances require technology coaches to apply what they have learned. However, these performances are usually limited to using technology in their own classroom practices, not helping other educators. For example, an approaches-level performance would be experimenting with online learning in their own classrooms but not helping other teachers to implement online learning in their classrooms (ISTE Standards•C, 3c).

While performances at the Approaches Level do not fully meet the ISTE Standards•C, they should not be underestimated. They are important prerequisites to becoming a technology coach. If individuals' performances at the Meets Level are lacking, studying the achievements under the Approaches Level can help them and their mentors identify gaps in foundational knowledge or emerging performances that need to be addressed.

University faculty who teach in programs aligned to the ISTE Standards•C should be aware that building foundational knowledge is a major component in candidates' course work. However, to receive accreditation, programs must show that their graduates are able to reach the Meets Level on the ISTE Standards•C rubric. This is usually accomplished through field experiences, field-based assignments, mentorship programs, and portfolios.

Meets Level

The Meets Level column of the rubric contains the ISTE Standards•C performance indicators that require technology coaches to apply their foundational knowledge and their classroom experiences. Demonstrating the skills and experiences necessary to help others is the hallmark of coaching. The most common verbs found at this performance level include "coach" and "model."

The following examples illustrate the Meets Level of the rubric:

- Coach teachers in and model design and implementation of technology-enhanced learning experiences addressing student content and technology literacy standards. (ISTE Standards•C, 2a)

- Model and facilitate safe, healthy, legal, and ethical uses of digital information and technologies. (ISTE Standards•C, 5b)

Exceeds Level

While the Meets Level of ISTE Standards•C is challenging, many experienced, dedicated technology coaches actually exceed this level on a regular basis. Exceeding standards requires coaches to use their highest level cognitive processes that demonstrably have influenced others' behaviors.

The Exceeds Level can be accomplished in the following ways:

- *Influence positive changes in others' practices.* Simply engaging in coaching activities does not guarantee that others will adopt new practices. Exemplary coaches can provide evidence they have helped their colleagues achieve new skills or perform at higher levels. Videos of classroom practice before and after teachers have received successful coaching is one powerful way to capture change.

- *Demonstrate that teachers' changed practices have resulted in enhanced student learning.* It is challenging to document student learning improvements, but there are ways to do it. In addition to achievement test results, improved learning can be documented through student products and projects. Student case studies or reflections are another way to show how technology has enhanced student learning. While it may take longer to gather this evidence, making positive impacts on students' learning should be the central goal of all educators.

- *Create resources that other technology coaches use.* Exemplary technology coaches are professionally active and respected by their peers. They produce resources that are used by other coaches. This might be as simple as sharing a training manual with another coach in the same district or as broad as mentoring other technology coaches around the world. Many coaches present at educational conferences and submit articles to professional journals.

- *Assume leadership responsibilities more common to technology directors.* The ISTE Standards•C require technology coaches to contribute to the development, communication, and implementation of organizational-level initiatives, but they do not require coaches to lead the initiatives. Moving beyond being a contributor to becoming a leader would be considered exemplary. These types of exemplary performances might be indicators that technology coaches are ready to assume responsibilities and perform tasks described in the ISTE Technology Director Standards (ISTE Standards•TD).

SUMMARY

The ISTE Standards•C rubric levels represent a logical progression toward exemplary performances for technology coaches. The following table will help distinguish among the Approaches, Meets, and Exceeds levels. Understanding the differences between and among these levels will help you better understand the rubric and the information contained in Chapters One through Six of this book.

TABLE I.1. Technology Coaching Rubric Levels

ISTE Standards•C Rubric Levels		
Approaches	**Meets**	**Exceeds**

• Contains sample performances that are important prerequisites for technology coaching, but do not quite meet the 28 ISTE Standards•C performance indicators.
 	
• Focuses on acquiring foundational knowledge related to technology coaching (examples: terms, principles, policies, issues, theories, strategies, tools, and best practices).
 	
• Generally addresses lower levels of cognitive skills. Standards most often begin with the words identify, define, and explain.
 	
• School-based performances focus on applying technology expertise in the technology coach's own classroom practice, not necessarily on helping others.
	• Contains the 28 ISTE Standards•C performance indicators
	
	• Focuses on applying foundational knowledge to help other educators use technology effectively.
	
	• Standards most often begin with the words coach and model.
	
	• Contains the 28 ISTE Standards•C performance indicators
	
	• Focuses on applying foundational knowledge to help other educators use technology effectively.
	
	• Standards most often begin with the words coach and model.
		• Contains sample performances that exceed the 28 performance indicators.
		
		• Focuses on performances that have high-level impact, including:
		
		  o Influencing positive changes in others' practices
		
		  o Improving students' learning as a direct result of coaching
		
		  o Producing coaching resources that are used by educators beyond their local school(s)
		
		  o Assuming technology leadership roles that exceed expectations of a technology coach.
		
		• Standards most often begin with these words: lead, produce resources, and provide evidence of change.

How Are the ISTE Standards•C Related to Other ISTE Standards?

The ISTE Standards•C belong to a family of ISTE standards for students, teachers, computer science educators, and administrators (ISTE Standards•S, ISTE Standards•T, ISTE Standards•CSE, and ISTE Standards•A). Each set of standards illuminates specific knowledge, skills, dispositions, and performances necessary to help students and educators thrive in the digital age. All of these standards can be found in Appendix A.

Since improved student learning is the primary goal of all educational efforts, the ISTE Standards•S are central to the ISTE Standards movement. The ISTE Standards•S describe what PK–12 students should understand and be able to do to learn effectively and live productively in an increasingly digital world. The standards are lofty learning goals, describing how students must leverage appropriate technologies to create, communicate, collaborate, and innovate. The ISTE Standards•S are used in many countries around the world and have been adopted, adapted, or referenced by most U.S. states. They also serve as the basis for student technology standards in schools and school districts. The importance of these standards continues to expand as technology literacy is increasingly addressed in high-profile assessments, such as the National Assessment for Educational Progress (NAEP) in the United States and the worldwide Programme for International Student Assessment (PISA), sponsored by the Organisation for Economic Co-operation and Development. (For more information on the NAEP, see http://nces.ed.gov/nationsreportcard; for more on PISA, see www.oecd.org/pisa/pisaproducts/pisa2015draftframeworks.htm.)

The ISTE Standards•T describe what classroom teachers must know and accomplish to fully implement new instructional paradigms. The assumptions underlying the Standards•T are different from long-standing beliefs that guide conventional educational practice. Digital age teachers need to change classrooms from teacher-centered, memory-focused environments to student-centered, performance-based settings where students engage in collaborative, authentic, real-world projects.

To achieve Standards•S and Standards•T, students and teachers need wholehearted support from administrators and hands-on assistance from tech coaches. The Standards•A and Standards•C describe what administrators and technology coaches must do to provide this support. Administrators, including principals and technology directors, focus on establishing a vision for technology in schools and systemic support for a digital age learning culture. Tech coaches contribute to the technology vision and help organizational members understand it. Coaches help teachers—and often administrators—learn about new technologies and implement them to improve student learning. The role of the tech coach is heavily oriented toward professional development. Helping teachers achieve Standards•T is the primary focus of the technology coach.

The ISTE standards are not a top-down construct. Teachers, technology coaches, and administrators work in concert to support student acquisition of Standards•S. Each group has a unique role to play, and in the best situations, they collaborate to learn from each other to enhance students' excitement about learning.

The Roles of Technology Coaches and Technology Directors

Technology coaches are those who work directly with teachers and often with students in schools to facilitate the effective use of technology for teaching, learning, and assessment. In contrast, technology directors are top-level administrators who lead technology programs at the district, state, regional, or national levels; they supervise tech coaches and ensure that they have the resources they need to do their work. As technology coaches advance in their careers, some may be asked to assume broader leadership responsibilities and may be called upon to become tech directors. Since technology directors are administrators, ISTE's Standards for Technology Directors are technically a part of the ISTE Standards for Administrators (ISTE Standards•A).

Technology coaches need to be aware that computer science educators have their own standards, ISTE Standards•CSE. These teachers have a special role in preparing students for the digital age, and tech coaches need to strongly support computer science teachers advance their mission. With their technical knowledge, computer science educators can be great partners for tech coaches to promote digital age literacy and skills.

How Are the ISTE Standards•C Related to ISTE Essential Conditions?

In addition to standards, ISTE has developed and published a list of Essential Conditions necessary to effectively leverage technology for learning. These 14 conditions describe cultural and environmental factors that support the full implementation of the ISTE standards. To achieve optimal digital age learning environments, all educators and stakeholders must reflect on these conditions, ensure they are in place, and strive to strengthen the conditions whenever possible. See the chart in Appendix B, which shows how the ISTE Essential Conditions are aligned with Standards•C.

The Essential Conditions have a multilayered, mutually beneficial connection with the ISTE Standards•C. The Essential Conditions point to the need for educational institutions to employ technology coaches and can be used to justify technology coaching positions. Exemplary technology coaches positively impact any organization's essential conditions on a daily basis.

Subsequent in this book will explore how technology coaches may strengthen the Essential Conditions as they implement the ISTE Standards•C. As you continue reading, look for the Essential Condition Connection boxes in Chapters One through Six.

ISTE Essential Conditions

The ISTE Essential Conditions are 14 critical elements necessary to effectively leverage technology for learning (www.iste.org/standards/essential-conditions).

Shared Vision

Proactive leadership develops a shared vision for educational technology among all education stakeholders, including teachers and support staff, school and district administrators, teacher educators, students, parents, and the community.

Empowered Leaders

Stakeholders at every level are empowered to be leaders in effecting change.

Implementation Planning

All stakeholders follow a systematic plan aligned with a shared vision for school effectiveness and student learning through the infusion of information and communication technology (ICT) and digital learning resources.

Consistent and Adequate Funding

Ongoing funding supports technology infrastructure, personnel, digital resources, and staff development.

Equitable Access

All students, teachers, staff, and school leaders have robust and reliable connectivity and access to current and emerging technologies and digital resources.

Skilled Personnel

Educators, support staff, and other leaders are skilled in the selection and effective use of appropriate ICT resources.

Ongoing Professional Learning

Educators have ongoing access to technology-related professional learning plans and opportunities as well as dedicated time to practice and share ideas.

Technical Support

Educators and students have access to reliable assistance for maintaining, renewing, and using ICT and digital learning resources.

Curriculum Framework

Content standards and related digital curriculum resources align with and support digital age learning and work.

Student-Centered Learning

Planning, teaching, and assessment all center on the needs and abilities of the students.

Assessment and Evaluation

Teaching, learning, leadership, and the use of ICT and digital resources are continually assessed and evaluated.

Engaged Communities

Leaders and educators develop and maintain partnerships and collaboration within the community to support and fund the use of ICT and digital learning resources.

Support Policies

Policies, financial plans, accountability measures, and incentive structures support the use of ICT and other digital resources for both learning and district/school operations.

Supportive External Context

Policies and initiatives at the national, regional, and local levels support schools and teacher preparation programs in the effective implementation of technology for achieving curriculum and learning technology (ICT) standards.

Why Are the ISTE Standards•C Important?

Technology coaches help individuals and entire organizations achieve ISTE's Essential Conditions and other ISTE standards. The actions of technology coaches are critical for achieving high-performance learning environments. By publishing the ISTE Standards•C, ISTE supports technology coaches in the following ways:

1. *Certifying, hiring, and retaining technology coaches.* Outlining what technology coaches should know and be able to do helps establish and communicate their importance. Technology coaching positions in education are relatively new when compared with those of principals, superintendents, teachers, media specialists, and curriculum directors. As a result, decision makers may not fully understand what technology coaches do. This lack of understanding is common when newer roles emerge in an organization. Educating stakeholders is an important first step in formalizing, justifying, and securing technology coaching positions in schools. Increased understanding is also important to ensure that technology coaches are awarded appropriate professional status, credibility, and compensation. Many organizations use professional standards as a basis for job descriptions, job postings, interview questions, and performance criteria. The ISTE Standards•C have helped states implement certification programs for technology coaches. Superintendents have used the ISTE Standards•C to help school board members understand how tech coaches are needed to shepherd their districts in to the digital age. When used for these purposes, ISTE Standards•C provide invaluable support for the hiring and continued employment of technology coaches in schools.

2. *Improving the performance of technology coaches.* The ISTE Standards•C provide practicing technology coaches with a framework to reflect on their own performances and identify areas where they need improvement. Reflections may prompt technology coaches to implement new strategies and seek professional learning opportunities. The ISTE Standards•C performances rubric provides additional opportunities for self-assessment. The rubric can also be adapted as a performance evaluation instrument.

3. *Recruiting and training future technology coaches.* The ISTE Standards•C provide a framework for graduate instructional technology programs that prepare future technology coaches. The Council for the Accreditation of Educational Programs (CAEP), the sole, specialized accreditation organization for educational programs in the United

States, has approved ISTE Standards • C. CAEP was formed through a consolidation of the National Council for Accreditation of Teacher Education (NCATE) and the Teacher Education Accreditation Council (TEAC) in 2013. When reviewing continuing education options, you can check to see if the program is aligned to the ISTE Standards • C. Reputable programs should be CAEP accredited or seeking CAEP accreditation.

ISTE STANDARDS•C IN ACTION

Opening Doors for Technology Coach Certification

—Traci Redish, Chair
Georgia Task Force on Instructional Technology
Standards and Certification

Several state education agencies in the United States offer certification for technology coaches, and the ISTE Standards•C have been influential in shaping that process. For example, the state of Georgia recently approved certification for instructional technology professionals who work in schools. The process began when a group of educators from school districts and universities took the ISTE Standards•C to the Georgia Professional Standards Commission (GaPSC) and asked if the commission would consider certifying technology coaches. These educators believed that certification would improve schools by empowering and formalizing technology coaching positions.

The GaPSC agreed to explore the option and formed a task force on instructional technology standards and certification. This panel of experts was charged with creating state standards to describe what technology coaches must know and be able to do. Instead of starting from scratch, the group decided to reference the ISTE Standards•C and use them as a starting point for drafting their own standards. After several months of writing and review, the first draft of the state instructional technology standards was nearly identical to the ISTE Standards•C. During an open review process, the proposed standards were overwhelmingly supported throughout the state and officially adopted by the GaPSC. Beginning in 2014, the state began offering instructional technology certification to educators who completed state-approved educational programs and demonstrated mastery of its new Instructional Technology standards.

As chair of the GaPSC Task Force, it was clear to me that ISTE Standards•C were critical to the state certification process. The instructional technology community had advocated for certification for many years, but in 2014, we were successful. As a set of internationally adopted professional standards, the ISTE Standards•C provided the credibility we needed to influence stakeholders and decision makers to pursue certification. The ISTE Standards•C also serve as a foundation for our new state standards. We hope that our story will inspire others to find ways to use the ISTE Standards•C to improve education in their states and organizations.

Who Should Know about the ISTE Standards•C?

The ISTE Standards•C define who technology coaches are, what they must know and be able to do, and why coaches are important. Because the standards serve to establish and validate the roles and responsibilities of technology coaches, several groups of people need to be familiar with them. This book is written with the following audiences in mind:

1. Educators who aspire to become technology coaches

2. Practicing technology coaches who want to improve and/or better understand their work

3. Educational leaders, such as principals, technology directors, superintendents, and school board members, who are responsible for hiring, evaluating, and retaining technology coaches

4. Parents and other key community stakeholders who need to understand and support technology coaching in schools

5. University faculty who prepare technology coaches through degree and certification programs

6. ISTE and CAEP reviewers who evaluate university graduate programs based on the ISTE Standards•C

7. Professional development providers who support the ongoing learning of technology coaches

8. Graduate students in ISTE Standards•C-aligned programs who are striving to show mastery of the standards in their course work, field experiences, and portfolios

9. Employees of state government agencies that provide certification to technology coaches

How Can I Learn More about the ISTE Standards•C?

As you continue to read this book, you will learn more about the ISTE Standards•C and how they can help you transform your school into a digital age learning environment that maximizes student engagement, motivation, and learning. Chapters One through Six address each standard individually. In each of these chapters you will find the following content:

- An in-depth explanation of each standard and supporting performance indicators

- Real-life case studies of how practicing technology coaches enacted some aspect of the ISTE Standards•C in their daily work

- A review of the ISTE Standards•C rubric for each standard

- Hypothetical scenarios describing what would be considered as approaching, meeting, and exceeding performances on the ISTE Standards•C rubric for each standard

- Resources aligned to each standard

- Discussion questions related to the standards

CHAPTER 1

Visionary Leadership

ISTE STANDARDS•C, STANDARD 1
Visionary Leadership

Technology coaches inspire and participate in the development and implementation of a shared vision for the comprehensive integration of technology to promote excellence and support transformational change throughout the instructional environment.

The first, most important standard for technology coaches is visionary leadership, establishing technology coaches as instrumental, creative educational leaders who help bring about positive, comprehensive changes in schools. Technology coaches help other educators envision how technology can enhance student learning. Technology coaches also participate in strategic planning and advocate for the resources necessary to transform shared visions into realities. Four elements relate to Standard One:

- Shared Vision

- Strategic Planning

- Advocacy

- Innovation and Change

Each element describes how technology coaches provide critical leadership support for technology programs in schools.

Shared Vision

ISTE STANDARDS•C, 1a
Shared Vision

Technology coaches contribute to the development, communication, and implementation of a shared vision for the comprehensive use of technology to support a digital age education for all students.

A vision describes an organization's ideal future—what the system members agree they would like to see happen over time. Formal vision statements are usually brief, aspirational, and long-term (at least five years from starting the visioning process). Having a shared vision for technology use is important because it sets a direction for technology coaching efforts and ensures that educators, students, parents, and community stakeholders agree on accomplishing the same goals that support the vision.

District administrators, with collaboration from faculty and staff members, are usually responsible for developing a vision. Technology coaches need to *contribute* to this vision. The representative committee that develops the vision gathers useful ideas by reviewing the professional literature and learning about best practices in other districts. Considering outside sources can inform, expand, and lend credibility to visionary ideas.

In addition to helping construct a vision, technology coaches also *communicate* the vision and help others *implement* the vision. Tech coaches and all vision committee members can share the organization's vision by talking to others about what it means, providing concrete examples of how it can be realized in practice, and helping other educators to implement visionary ideas. In these ways, technology coaches can familiarize their colleagues with new ideas, helping them focus on the vision until it becomes a reality.

Strategic Planning

ISTE STANDARDS•C, 1b
Strategic Planning

Technology coaches contribute to the planning, development, communication, implementation, and evaluation of technology-infused strategic plans at the district and/or school levels.

To achieve a shared vision for technology use in schools, individuals at all levels need to participate in strategic planning. When strategic plans are made only by top administrators or small commitees, it's not surprising that many teachers and staff members feel as if the plans have nothing to do with them. Some organizations integrate technology-related strategies in their organizational-level strategic plans. Others have separate, more detailed technology plans. Many organizations do both. Whatever form these technology plans take, they will include goals, strategies, timelines, budgets, and responsibility lists. Good plans also contain evaluation components to gauge how well goals are being met.

Technology directors may be responsible for collaboratively developing plans via broad-based planning with key stakeholders including teachers and parents. Technology coaches are expected to *contribute* to the planning, development, implementation, and evaluation of plans. Technology coaches' input to planning is invaluable because they work closely with teachers, students, and principals. Technology coaches are in perfect positions to ascertain

Strategic Planning Glossary

Terminology related to strategic planning often varies across organizations, but here are some generally accepted definitions. These definitions will be helpful to technology coaches participating in technology planning or advocating for the inclusion of technology in system-level strategic plans.

Vision. A vision describes what an organization hopes to achieve in an ideal future, within five to seven years beyond the planning period. Visions are usually represented in a brief, inspirational, aspirational statement of approximately three to seven sentences. Vision statements are *visual*. They describe what an observer would see in the future. The best visions are concrete, not abstract, and they answer the question: What should the future look like? When the vision is specific, community members understand what they can do to help the school district move closer to everyone's shared vision. Good vision statements move beyond what types of technologies should be purchased. The vision should focus on digital-age skills, student achievement of content standards, and the technology-supported classroom practices that will help achieve those goals. An effective, practical vision will show people why achieving the vision is important by illustrating how the technologies will turn the vision into reality.

Mission Statement. During planning, some organizations—or departments within organizations—also develop mission statements. Mission statements are usually shorter than vision statements, from one to three sentences long. While vision statements focus on the future, mission statements describe the fundamental purposes of the organization and why it exists. Some mission statements also communicate the core values of the organization and how those values influence the mission.

External Scan. External scanning usually refers to an analysis of the larger context in which the organization operates. During external scans, leaders and system members search for innovations, best practices, and research findings relevant to the plan. External scanning also includes an analysis of the current and future social, economic, and political landscape and how these factors will likely impact the organization. These activities stretch the community's thinking and help produce high-quality plans that are response, proactive, and informed.

Goals. Goals can be specific, tangible, and measurable, or they can express a more general intent. In all cases, goals are more specific and shorter term than a vision. Goals describe a result or particular outcomes that are attainable during the time frame of the plan.

Objectives. Objectives are not used in every plan, but they are helpful and necessary when goals are broad in scope and not measurable. Objectives are more narrow, precise, tangible, and concrete than goals. Unlike broad goals, objectives are measurable and can be validated when achieved.

Benchmarks. Like objectives, benchmarks are not used in every plan, but they are helpful in some cases. Benchmarks are intermediate checkpoints to measure progress toward an end goal or objective. They fall between the launch of the plan and the end of the plan. Benchmarks are often used as related to student achievement when measuring student performance compared to an established standard.

Strategies. Planners frequently confuse goals, objectives, and benchmarks with strategies, but the difference is clear. Strategies are activities that planners hope will *lead* to the desired goals, objectives, and/or benchmarks. Strategy statements frequently begin with action verbs that describe what a person or group will do. Since strategies require resources to implement, they are usually accompanied by budgets, timelines, and responsibility lists.

which goals are necessary and practical. Tech coaches are likely to become responsible for implementing many strategies in the plan, especially those related to professional development. Technology coaches can also provide formative feedback on how the plan is working and help technology directors modify strategies because they are immersed in day-to-day practice. Coaches may also gather data to evaluate how the plan is meeting students' and teachers' needs.

First, tech coaches need to understand strategic plans, and then they can serve as indispensable bridges between those who create organization's plans and the needs of local schools' teachers and students. Through conversations with educators at all levels, tech coaches can glean useful insights into the planning process. To become effective contributors, technology coaches also need to read existing strategic plans and learn how plans are developed and implemented.

Strategic Process for Constructing a Technology Plan

Technology directors or other tech-savvy administrators are usually responsible for leading technology planning. The following are the accepted components of a strategic planning process, even though organizations vary and planning is usually not quite as linear as depicted here. Technology coaches can benefit from a basic understanding of planning in two ways. First, understanding the planning process will help them learn how to participate and contribute to their organization's technology plan. Second, they can use some of these processes to lead planning initiatives with small groups of teachers in their schools.

Professional strategic planners have learned that each of the following steps needs to be followed completely and in the order given. Skipping a step or racing through a step too quickly can result in miscommunications among stakeholders and loss of time in the long term.

SIX STEPS OF THE PLANNING PROCESS

1. **Preplanning.** The first step the planning process is preplanning—a time-consuming phase often underestimated by planners. At this stage, leaders design the planning process, develop a timeline for creating the plan, identify key stakeholders who should be invited to participate, and list any local issues likely to influence planning. To plan effectively, leaders and participants need to be familiar with previous technology plans and other strategic planning initiatives to which technology planning must be aligned. Preplanning should include a discussion of why the proposed plan is necessary. Whereas the need to integrate technology into instruction may seem self-evident to technology specialists, it may not be as clear to other stakeholders or critics. Technology planners should be prepared present rationales, including how technology can improve student learning, equip students with technology literacy skills, and meet the needs and preferences of digital age learners.

2. **Community Visioning.** Next, planners need to lead stakeholders in a collaborative, democratic, community visioning process. Ideally, visioning should involve as many stakeholders as possible, and participants should represent each segment of the community with connections to schools, including businesses, law enforcement, and social services, as well as parents and students. To inform visioning, participants need to perform broad external scans to compile current research, best practices, and innovations that will inform the vision. When stakeholders gather and share fresh ideas, they are

better able to make informed decisions. Technology planners need to be highly skilled in helping large groups of individuals to understand, evaluate, and synthesize large quantities of information along with many individuals' ideas. If planners navigate this stage well, stakeholders are more likely to create a concise, inclusive vision statement. Most technology plans' vision statements range between three to seven sentences, that is, one concise paragraph.

3. **Assessing Current Reality/Needs.** After the planning group has constructed a vision statement, planners frequently ask the community stakeholders in the group to assess the distance between current reality and the new vision. By reflecting together, the group identifies essential conditions for realizing their preferred future. This step, often referred to as a gap analysis or needs assessment, is best accomplished collaboratively, so that it represents the needs of the community as a whole. Basing the needs assessment on data collected from sources such as equipment inventories, observations, surveys, interviews, focus groups, and student achievement information makes it easier for planners to justify requests that require additional funding. Once the planning group determines the community's needs, the group can go to the next stage of the process.

4. **Constructing Goals and Evaluation Plan.** Because needs usually outpace available resources, stakeholders must prioritize current needs and establish some goals that are achievable during the time frame covered in the plan. Goals, with or without supporting objectives, should be stated in terms of desirable, measurable outcomes. An evaluation plan accompanies the list of goals and describes how progress toward each goal will be measured and reported. Anyone reading the list of goals along with the evaluation plan should be able to understand what constitutes each goal's successful accomplishment. In some scenarios, particular data collected for the needs assessment can serve as a baseline for evaluating future progress. If so, these data are included as parts of the evaluation plan.

5. **Action Planning.** In addition to goals and an evaluation plan, planners also need to construct an action plan. The action plan consists of strategies that will help the stakeholders reach their goals. Common strategies include purchasing equipment, implementing professional development, and offering incentives for desirable actions. For a plan to be complete, each of its strategies needs to be accompanied by budgets, timelines, and responsibility lists. Novice planners often begin and end with action planning, but that is unwise as well as unproductive. To undertake action planning without preplanning and then creating a shared vision, goals, and an evaluation plan wastes time because the group will have to go back to work through the skipped steps. Each of these planning steps needs to be followed in this order to ensure that all stakeholders work together toward the same vision—in so doing, they will take ownership of the entire process.

6. **Marketing and Communicating the Plan.** A marketing and communication plan helps ensure that the Technology Plan doesn't sit on a shelf. Communicating and marketing activities build support for the plan and make sure that the whole community understands and implements it. Sharing ongoing updates and evaluation findings helps stakeholders monitor progress, make necessary refinements, and celebrate successes. In so far as tech coaches help people in the broader community understand the need for a technology plan, the vision and goals toward enacting it, and progress toward reaching it, coaches function as invaluable assets.

TECHNOLOGY COACHING CASE STUDY

Visioning, Planning, and Piloting

—Nancy Johnson
Fifth Grade Teacher
GREENWOOD ELEMENTARY SCHOOL
WAUKEGAN, ILLINOIS

ISTE STANDARDS•C, 1a. Technology coaches contribute to the development, communication, and implementation of a shared vision for the comprehensive use of technology to support a digital age education for all students.

ISTE STANDARDS•C, 1b. Contribute to the planning, development, communication, implementation, and evaluation of technology-infused strategic plans at the district and school levels.

Fifth grade teacher Nancy Johnson says she became an unofficial technology coach by accident. "Let me put it this way," Nancy explained. "I always want the newest technology available. Getting the technology first usually comes with the stipulation that I figure things out and then help others learn."

Because of her willingness to try new things and help others, Johnson is well-known as a teacher-technology leader throughout her school district. Most recently, Johnson was asked to serve as the only elementary teacher on a district-wide planning committee to design digital age classrooms.

Before planning district-wide, digital age classrooms, the committee decided to pilot the design in a single classroom. The purposes of the pilot include testing the selected technologies and gathering examples of how the technologies can be used to support instruction. The committee asked Johnson to implement the pilot. She agreed.

Johnson's classroom was gutted from ceiling to floor. The room now has new furniture for a learning-center design, five desktops, interactive TV, an amplification system, and an iPad. She is documenting her students' and her own successes and challenges for the planning committee. Johnson is also learning how best to use the room so that she can help other teachers when their classrooms change.

Throughout this process, she believes her greatest contributions to the committee include her knowledge of curriculum, classroom practices, and how technology can support learning. She advocated for an environment to fit flexible grouping and multimedia-rich environments she believes all digital age learners need.

"Overall, I believe our current design is meeting the committee's goals—except we need more iPads. I am pretty sure I can negotiate a classroom set if I promise to teach others how to use them," Johnson smiled.

Advocacy

ISTE STANDARDS•C, 1c
Advocacy

Technology coaches advocate for policies, procedures, programs, and funding strategies to support the implementation of the shared vision represented in the school and district technology plans and guidelines.

Exemplary technology coaches are passionate *advocates* for using technology to improve teaching and learning. They make recommendations and actively support policies, procedures, and practices that advance instructional technology programs. They also are willing to speak out against actions that would impede progress.

Technology-related advocacy efforts can occur on many levels. Advocacy can be as simple as asking the principal or district technology director to provide needed equipment, supplies, or professional development opportunities. On a larger scale, it can involve explaining the need for technology-related programs to superintendents, school board members, and legislators. Because technology coaches work closely with teachers and students the stories they tell can be powerful, persuasive advocacy tools.

To become effective advocates, technology coaches must understand the district, state, and national policies and programs that affect local technology efforts. They also need to know how decisions are made and how they can appropriately and effectively make their voices heard during the process.

TECHNOLOGY COACHING CASE STUDY

Advocating All the Time

—Caroline Haebig
Instructional Technology Coordinator
ADLAI E. STEVENSON HIGH SCHOOL
LINCOLNSHIRE, ILLINOIS

ISTE STANDARDS•C, 1c. Advocate for policies, procedures, programs, and funding strategies to support implementation of the shared vision represented in the school and district technology plans and guidelines.

Caroline Haebig is an Apple Distinguished Educator and an Indiana University School of Education Jacobs Teacher Educator Award recipient for inquiry-based learning. She has also received the ISTE Outstanding Young Educator Award. Haebig taught high school social studies in Kenosha, Wisconsin; now, she serves as the instructional technology coordinator at Adlai E. Stevenson High School in Lincolnshire, IL. She attributes her success to sharing her classroom innovations with others and advocating for the resources and conditions that make innovation possible.

Haebig defines advocacy broadly, and saying it permeates nearly every aspect of her professional practice. When teaching, she made videos of what students were doing and shared them. She even engages in what she calls "everyday advocacy" at the gym, grocery store, or anywhere she can cast technology as essential and not a luxury or an add-on.

When Wisconsin faced severe budget cuts to education, she learned to advocate on a broader scale. Fearful that cuts would endanger teachers' professional learning, pay increases for advanced degrees, and money for technology purchases, she protested on weekends, sent emails, and met with legislators face to face.

Even though the budget cuts were passed, Haebig believes her role made a difference: "Legislators need our stories and perspectives. It's important to encourage legislators and say thank you. It's not about winning or losing; it is about the process, being informed, energizing the conversation, and being involved."

Haebig encourages all technology coaches to be advocates and suggests they connect with professional organizations, such as the International Society for Technology in Education (ISTE), that post updates and provide contact information to policymakers. Haebig also stresses the importance of connecting to state ISTE affiliates and watching local decision making.

"People often neglect local activity," says Haebig, "but this is really where we have the greatest chance of making a difference. The best kind of advocacy is positive, personal, and ongoing. It builds the type of deep community support that prevents undesirable situations."

Innovation and Change

ISTE STANDARDS•C, 1d
Innovation and Change

Technology coaches implement strategies for initiating and sustaining technology innovations and manage the change process in schools and classrooms.

Like all effective educational leaders, technology coaches are well versed in *initiating, sustaining,* and *managing* the change process in organizations. Theory and research suggest that technology innovations with a high-degree of alignment to current instructional practices have the best chance for adoption. Yet, the educational technology practices described in the ISTE Standards for Students (ISTE Standards•S) call for a shift toward more student-centered, inquiry-based models of instruction. Because of this, technology coaches may find themselves facilitating the most difficult type of instructional change—the type that challenges some educators' long-standing beliefs about teaching and learning. When technology coaches work with this type of transformation, they are likely to encounter questions, anxiety, frustration, and even resistance from their colleagues.

To manage such difficult situations, technology coaches must comprehend how transformative change occurs. Once technology coaches understand typical human behavior during transformations, they are better equipped to help their colleagues become supportive of the change process. In doing so, they strengthen the likelihood that their fellow educators will adopt learning technologies and use them effectively.

Technology coaches can improve their understanding of how people react to proposed transformations by studying theories of change, especially those related to educational settings or the adoption of innovations. Learning from experienced technology coaches and other educational leaders can also be helpful. Experienced and exemplary technology coaches have a vast repertoire of strategies to use when challenges arise.

Excellent tech coaches are skillful change agents who help other educators see the need to adopt new tools and techniques. The effective integration of new technologies into teaching and learning would be unlikely, if not impossible, without the instructional, technical, and emotional support that coaches provide to other educators.

TECHNOLOGY COACHING CASE STUDY

Using Force Multipliers to Support the District's Vision

—David Beard
Sixth through Eighth Grade Technology Training Specialist
DYSART UNIFIED SCHOOL DISTRICT
SURPRISE, ARIZONA

ISTE STANDARDS•C, 1a. Contribute to the development, communication, and implementation of a shared vision for the comprehensive use of technology to support a digital age education for all students.

ISTE STANDARDS•C, 1d. Implement strategies for initiat ing and sustaining technology innovations and manage the change process in schools and classrooms.

David Beard's school district is well-known for technology leadership and a cutting-edge vision for technology and learning. Among other honors, the district was selected as a National School Board Association Technology Site Visit in 2012.

To help others understand and implement the district's vision, Beard must constantly manage and support changes in middle school classrooms located in 20 schools. To address this challenge, Beard identifies and empowers what he calls "force multipliers," that is, talented individuals of all ages who can best help him spread the vision to others.

For example, each school has an innovation ambassador, a full-time teacher who uses technology effectively in his or her classroom and receives a stipend for helping others before or after school. Each school also employs a full-time instructional growth teacher dedicated to teachers' professional development. Since Beard cannot possibly have direct contact with all teachers, he concentrates on supporting the innovation ambassadors and instructional growth teachers who help him spread new ideas.

Beard also coaches small groups of teacher-selected student leaders on how to use technologies to complete projects. In turn, these students teach what they've learned to other students and their teachers. Beard believes students are powerful forces for change. He also believes training students relieves pressure on teachers and supports student-centered learning, as represented in the district's vision.

"It is most productive to see my job as building capacity for change rather than directly influencing each individual teacher and student," explains Beard. "I am willing to help anyone, but to get the job done, I have to enlist the help of force multipliers any way I can."

Exemplary Performance in Visionary Leadership

The ISTE Technology Coaching Rubric describes performances that approach, meet, and exceed expectations for visionary leadership (ISTE Standards•C, 1a–d). This section explains the rubric as related to Standard One and provides more examples in each category.

Table 1.1 illustrates how coaches can have positive effects on visionary leadership. Note the differences in performances among the approaches, meets, and exceeds levels.

APPROACHES

To achieve the performance level termed *approaches* for Visionary Leadership, technology coaches will be able to define terms and basic concepts related to shared visions, strategic planning, advocacy, and change. They will also be able to explain why these four elements are important to advancing effective technology use in schools. These performances are important for leadership preparation; however, tech coaches who have just met the *approaches* level stop short of actually influencing technology planning, policies, and implementation in schools.

The following Rubric Scenarios offer examples of performances best described as the *approaches* level toward meeting the Visionary Leadership expectations for technology coaches:

Merideth is a full-time teacher recognized at her school for helping her colleagues use technology in their classrooms. Recently, she became aware that her school district had a shared vision and a strategic plan for technology use. Someday she would like to participate in developing that plan, but for now, she is studying the plan and looking at plans in other districts. She asked her principal how the vision and the plan were constructed. The principal explained the process to Merideth, volunteered to introduce her to the district's technology director, and sent an email recommending her as a member of the district's technology planning committee.

Seth is a full-time technology coach serving three elementary schools in a district. He feels he's well prepared to help teachers in the classroom, but he doesn't know much about strategic planning. At technology department meetings, the technology director and other technology coaches have been using some terms that are a bit unfamiliar to him. To increase his knowledge, he is reading some credible resources on strategic planning and determining how vision statements, goals, and strategies differ. He also asked to observe the district's strategic planning committee to learn more about how plans are collaboratively constructed.

Karen is a teacher and a graduate student in instructional technology. One of her assignments is to explore how technology might best support teaching and learning. Once she has completed this research, she will write a paper describing how she would like to see technology used in schools over the next five years. The paper will also include a rationale explaining why she thinks her recommendations will lead schools in the best direction. The assignment is titled "Personal Technology Vision Paper."

Tamera is a middle school principal who wants to make sure she is maximizing all funding sources for technology. To begin, she is researching how technology is funded for her school and what local, state, and federal programs are available to her school. She is also exploring how private organizations and partnerships might be able to provide additional resources.

Clarissa is a first-year technology coach who is excited about helping others use technology, but as she began to meet her colleagues, she was surprised that some resisted her suggestions about how they could change their traditional practices. Other technology coaches explained that her colleagues' reactions were normal and suggested Clarissa might want to seek some professional development courses to help her learn how to navigate the change process. Clarissa signed up for a six-week leadership seminar through her regional office of education. In this class, she is reading theories of change and engages in online discussions with other educational leaders. She is also observing some of her fellow technology coaches as they work with teachers who are cautious about implementing new practices.

MEETS

A tech coach who meets expectations for Visionary Leadership has moved beyond the mastery of informational and preparatory activities. To meet Standard One, technology coaches must actually *contribute* to the development, communication, implementation, and/or evaluation of shared visions or strategic plans for instructional technology. Similarly, they must show evidence of engaging in *advocacy* efforts and *supporting change* initiatives in schools.

The following rubric scenarios offer examples of individuals' performances best described as *meeting* the Visionary Leadership expectations for technology coaches:

Kevin is an experienced, full-time technology coach who serves on the district technology planning committee. As the committee began its work to construct a new plan, he participated in a group brainstorming session to create a shared vision for technology use in the district's schools. For a long time, Kevin thought that his school would benefit from a vision that stressed student-centered uses of technology. Therefore, he proposed using technology to support cross-site collaboration, global awareness, creativity, and innovation.

Yasmeen is a media specialist who believes in the district technology vision and plan but realized that not many teachers in her school knew about the plan. At first she shared the vision statement with them, but she was a little disappointed in their responses. She felt like the teachers were supportive of the vision but didn't know what it really meant. Therefore, Yasmeen asked the principal if she could use the first five minutes of every staff meeting to show a video of classroom technology use that aligned with the district's vision. She called the videos "Vision to Practice Examples."

Theresa is a teacher who loves learning about technology. She has been reading about exemplary technology practices across the country, especially 1:1 and Bring Your Own Device (BYOD) programs. Thinking that her district might want to move in this direction, she emailed some of these resources to the district technology staff. She asked them to consider 1:1 initiatives in her school, and she volunteered to pilot a 1:1 implementation in her classroom—just in case the opportunity arises!

Caroline is a part-time teacher and part-time technology coach. The technology director asked Caroline how to increase participation in the technology planning process.

TABLE 1.1. Technology Coaching Rubric for Standard 1

Standard 1. Visionary Leadership

Technology coaches inspire and participate in the development and implementation of a shared vision for the comprehensive integration of technology to promote excellence and support transformational change throughout the instructional environment.

a. **Shared Vision.** Contribute to the development, communication, and implementation of a shared vision for the comprehensive use of technology to support a digital age education for all students.

b. **Strategic Planning.** Contribute to the planning, development, communication, implementation, and evaluation of technology-infused strategic plans at the district and/or school levels.

c. **Advocacy.** Advocate for policies, procedures, programs, and funding strategies to support the implementation of the shared vision represented in the school and district technology plans and guidelines.

d. **Innovation and Change.** Implement strategies for initiating and sustaining technology innovations and manage the change process in schools and classrooms.

Approaches	Meets	Exceeds
TECHNOLOGY COACHES:	TECHNOLOGY COACHES:	TECHNOLOGY COACHES:
• Define the term shared vision and explain the importance of developing, communicating, and implementing a shared vision for technology use in schools and strategic plans to reach the vision. (1a) • Analyze how the content of national, state, and local strategic plans currently support the effective use of technology in schools. (1b) • Identify strategies to advocate for policies, procedures, programs, and funding strategies to support the implementation of a shared vision as represented in the school and district technology plans and guidelines. (1c) • Identify principles of organizational change and project management useful when initiating and sustaining effective use of technology innovations in K–12 schools. (1d)	• Contribute to the development, communication, and implementation of a shared vision for the comprehensive use of technology to support a digital age education for all students. (1a) • Contribute to the planning, development, communication, implementation, and evaluation of technology-infused strategic plans at the district and/or school levels. (1b) • Advocate for policies, procedures, programs, and funding strategies to support the implementation of the shared vision represented in the school and district technology plans and guidelines. (1c) • Implement strategies for initiating and sustaining technology innovations and manage the change process in schools and classrooms. (1d)	• Lead school-level teams in developing, communicating, and/or implementing a shared vision for the comprehensive use of technology to support a digital age education for all students. (1a) • Lead school-level teams in planning, developing, communicating, implementing, and evaluating technology-infused strategic plans. (1b) • Lead advocacy activities resulting in improved policies, procedures, programs, and/or funding strategies to support the shared vision represented in school and/or district technology plans and guidelines. (1c) • Design innovative strategies for initiating and sustaining technology innovations and manage the change process in schools and classrooms. (1d) • Provide evidence of improved teaching and learning as a result of helping others successfully adopt/adapt technology innovations. (1a–d) • Produce resources related to shared visioning, strategic planning, advocacy, and innovations/changes that are used by educators beyond the local school. (1a–d)

Caroline proposed an online discussion forum where all educators, parents, and students can post scenarios of how they hope technology can be used in the future. The technology director loved the idea. Caroline creates, tests, and provides feedback on the forum's discussions.

Caleb is a teacher who works diligently to integrate technology into his teaching in engaging, meaningful ways, but the way that technology is organized in his classroom doesn't fit his teaching style. There are six computers connected to the district's local area network in the back of his room. When he wants groups of students to use computers at the same time, it is very crowded and noisy. All 30 students are huddled into a small space while the rest of the room is empty. Caleb would take his class to the computer lab, but the lab is frequently being used for testing or scheduled by other teachers. Caleb has been working with his school's tech coach to advocate for six laptops that can connect to a wireless network instead of desktop computers that must stay stationary. He believes that laptops would also help his colleagues maximize their classrooms' space, allow for flexible grouping, and support outside inquiry projects in the school's green space. Caleb, assisted by his tech coach, have written a proposal explaining how the laptops would help his students learn more effectively, and the coach believes the proposal is likely to be accepted during the next year, when it will be time to refresh equipment.

Adisa is a full-time technology coach to several schools. In response to one of her grant proposals, the schools she serves received a large government grant to improve education using technology. She frequently writes letters telling funders—local business owners as well as governmental sources—stories of how technology is helping students and thanking them for their continued support of the growing technology program.

Mickey is a technology coach who knows that the change process involves answering people's questions. However, he also knows that many teachers avoid asking questions in large groups or posting them on discussion forums for all to see. Therefore, he makes once-a-month visits to grade-level team meetings. He doesn't plan an agenda or take a lot of time, but he answers questions and leaves a tech newsletter he writes with every group. To make sure he is always welcome, he limits his time to no more than ten minutes and brings the teachers a snack. He also maintains individual relationships with teachers so they feel comfortable asking him questions between meetings.

EXCEEDS

Technology coaches *exceed* expectations for Visionary Leadership when they begin to assume roles usually expected of technology directors and other top-level school administrators. Exceeding performances can also include *leading* or having great successes in *advocacy* or change initiatives. Producing leadership resources that are used by others is another way to distinguish excellent technology coaching performance.

The following rubric scenarios offer examples of performances best described as *exceeding* the Visionary Leadership expectations for technology coaches:

Cassie is an instructional technology graduate student who studied technology leadership and completed several course projects related to technology planning. When she shared her work with her principal, he asked her to lead a committee of teachers to infuse technology into their school-level strategic plan. She organized groups, called for volunteers, and spent the next year revising the plan to include technology-related goals and strategies.

Viktor is one of 10 technology coaches in his medium-sized district. When his district engages in technology planning, the coaches host a large, open meeting to gather input from teachers, students, parents, and community stakeholders. In preparation for the meeting, the district technology director asked Viktor to create a 10-minute multimedia presentation about what is happening with instructional technology across the world. The video, designed to stretch people's thinking about what is possible, was shown at the meeting. Viktor introduced the video and explained its purpose. Then, he served as a facilitator for one of the table groups. His role was to keep the group on task, record ideas, and present a report of the group's ideas.

Carmen is a technology coach who is active in professional organizations related to technology. As part of her service to one group, she keeps track of state and federal legislation that could harm or benefit technology programs in schools. She also manages an email list of members who have asked to receive news on technology-related issues. Carmen sends them legislative updates and suggestions on how to participate in advocacy efforts sponsored by the professional organization.

Marah is a full-time technology coach. In her district, the technology plan calls for using new data software for tracking students' progress and differentiating learning. The strategy related to this goal was to provide two hands-on training sessions for each school; however, teachers were still not using the software after training. Marah suggested that she make appointments with each grade-level and content area team to model the process with their current students. The technology director reorganized Marah's work time to implement this new strategy. As she continued to work with each team, teachers begin using the new software and designing new instructional strategies for students who weren't achieving. Over time, Marah was able to present data showing that teachers who are using the new software and differentiating instruction have increased student achievement.

Robert is a technology coach in a school that successfully implemented a 1:1 initiative. Because the implementation was successful, others began asking him for advice. Robert believes that a big part of their success was long-range planning for the initiative. One year prior to the implementation, he designed and led a summer planning session where teachers envisioned what a 1:1 classroom would look like, what they could do when students had access to personal devices, and how to manage the 1:1 environment. Over the following year, teachers planned and shared curriculum materials. By the time students were issued laptops, the teachers were prepared. Robert documented the process and put his facilitation guides online for other districts to use. He has shared the planning process at several conferences, and others have replicated the program.

Discussion Questions for Visionary Leadership

1. What is the vision for technology use in your organization? How many system members are able to articulate the vision clearly? How many agree with the vision? What could be done to help more people adopt the vision?

2. What types of strategic plans exist in your organization? Is there an overarching strategic plan and a separate technology plan? Or does the organization's strategic plan include technology-related components? What are the pros and cons of having a separate technology plan versus a strategic plan with an embedded technology plan? Is technology adequately represented in the organization's primary plan?

3. What is the planning process in your organization? How can you become involved in that process? If you could be involved, how would you like the planning process or the content of the plans to change? How can you prepare yourself to participate in local technology planning efforts?

4. In the United States, various funding programs and policies contributed to widespread technology planning at the national, state, and school district levels, but technology planning at the individual school level is rarer. At what levels do you think technology planning is needed? Do you think schools need individual technology plans? Why or why not?

5. How will the process and content differ among national, state, district, and school-level technology plans? Should there be any alignment of planning efforts among these different levels? Provide a rationale for your answers.

6. What does advocacy mean to you? Provide an example of when you were an advocate. How can you be a more effective advocate for technology use in schools?

7. How do you think organizational change occurs? What readings or experiences have influenced your opinions? What are some strategies that technology coaches can use to positively influence desirable changes? What challenges will technology coaches likely encounter, and how can they address these challenges? What change strategies have you used to successfully foster positive change? Do you think adopting new technologies is different from other types of change initiatives? Why or why not?

Resources for Visionary Leadership

WEBSITES

ISTE Standards for Students (ISTE Standards•S)
www.iste.org/standards/standards-for-students
The ISTE Standards for students are the first place to start when developing a shared vision for technology use in classrooms. These standards reflect the knowledge and skills that students need for work, life, and citizenship in a digital age with a global economy. The ISTE Standards•S are lofty learning goals, describing how students must leverage appropriate technologies to create, communicate, collaborate, and innovate.

ISTE Essential Conditions
www.iste.org/standards/essential-conditions
To assist educators in planning successful technology initiatives, ISTE has published a list of essential conditions necessary to leverage technology for learning. These essential conditions can serve as a framework for reflection and planning. Good technology plans address all 14 essential conditions to increase the likelihood of successful technology programs. On ISTE's website, users can select each essential condition for an in-depth definition, as well as a discussion of why each condition is important and what it looks like in practice.

Essential Conditions Connection—ISTE Essential Conditions and Standards•C, Standard 1

One could argue that technology coaches support all the essential conditions when they implement ISTE Standards•C, Standard One–Visionary Leadership. Certainly, during the planning process, leaders must assess and plan for activities in all 14 condition areas. However, some essential conditions are addressed more directly than others. These conditions include the following:

- **Shared Vision**
- **Empowered Leaders**
- **Implementation Planning**
- **Consistent and Adequate Funding**
- **Assessment and Evaluation**
- **Engaged Communities**
- **Support Policies**
- **Supportive External Context**

TABLE 1.2. ISTE Essential Conditions Related to ISTE Standards•C, 1

ISTE Essential Conditions	ISTE STANDARDS•C 1. Visionary Leadership
SHARED VISION Proactive leadership develops a shared vision for educational technology among all education stakeholders, including teachers and support staff, school and district administrators, teacher educators, students, parents, and the community.	Shared Vision (ISTE Standards•C, 1a) When technology coaches help develop and/or disseminate a shared vision for technology use, they are supporting this important essential condition. Both the ISTE Standards•C and the ISTE Essential Conditions highlight the importance of collaboratively constructing a community-based vision.
EMPOWERED LEADERS Stakeholders at every level are empowered to be leaders in effecting change.	Innovation and Change (ISTE Standards•C, 1d) When technology coaches are leaders who make change happen, they introduce and facilitate the effective use of technology-supported teaching innovations. They are critical change agents who support others in navigating the change process. They provide technical and emotional support for instructional transformation.
IMPLEMENTATION PLANNING All stakeholders follow a systematic plan aligned with a shared vision for school effectiveness and student learning through the infusion of information and communication technology (ICT) and digital learning resources.	Strategic Planning (ISTE Standards•C, 1b) Technology coaches contribute to the planning, development, and communication of strategic plans that support technology use in schools.

Table continued on next page

Table continued from previous page

CONSISTENT AND ADEQUATE FUNDING Ongoing funding supports technology infrastructure, personnel, digital resources, and staff development.	Strategic Planning (ISTE Standards•C, 1b) Advocacy (ISTE Standards•C, 1c) When helping to construct strategic plans, technology coaches advocate for the funding needed to advance technology-supported teaching and learning.
ASSESSMENT AND EVALUATION Teaching, learning, leadership, and the use of ICT and digital resources are continually assessed and evaluated.	Strategic Planning (ISTE Standards•C, 1b) Good strategic plans include both formative and summative evaluation activities to monitor progress. Technology coaches help design and implement these evaluation measures.
SUPPORT POLICIES Policies, financial plans, accountability measures, and incentive structures support the use of ICT and other digital resources for learning and district/school operations.	ISTE Standards•C, 1b - Strategic Planning ISTE Standards•C, 1c – Advocacy Constructing strategic plans involves creating policies, financial plans, accountability measures, and incentive structures. In the planning process, technology coaches frequently advocate for policies and programs that maximize the effective use of technology for instructional and school business operations. Because of their proximity to practice, they are able to help create policy and programs that are practical and responsive to classroom-level needs.
SUPPORTIVE EXTERNAL CONTEXT Policies and initiatives at the national, regional, and local levels support schools and teacher preparation programs in the effective implementation of technology for achieving curriculum and learning technology standards.	ISTE Standards•C, 1c – Advocacy External factors can enable or impede local technology programs. Technology coaches are informed educators who advocate for policies and initiatives that improve teaching and learning through the use of technology.

ISTE Lead & Transform Diagnostic Tool
www.iste.org/lead/lead-transform/diagnostic-tool
The ISTE Lead & Transform Diagnostic Tool is a free resource that takes a snapshot of a school's or district's alignment to the 14 Essential Conditions for learning and teaching with technology. The tool generates a free report with data that can guide tech planning and implementation decisions. The questionnaire takes approximately 20 to 40 minutes to complete.

Edutopia Videos
www.edutopia.org
Videos published on the Edutopia website are funded by the George Lucas Foundation for Education. They are excellent resources to help educators envision new possibilities for education. Not all the videos focus on technology use, but many do. Search features help users find specific topics. Use these videos and other Edutopia resources to stretch your own thinking and to inspire those you coach.

Project Tomorrow
www.tomorrow.org
Project Tomorrow is a U.S. not-for-profit organization that conducts an annual survey on critical issues of digital age education. The survey is open to all students, parents, and educators. The results are provided to state and national policy makers. School and district-level technology planners also find the results interesting. Survey results can stimulate interesting discussions when educators envision how technology can enhance education.

E-rate Technology Plan Guidance
www.usac.org/sl/applicants/step01/default.aspx
The federal E-rate program provides U.S. schools and libraries with discounts for telecommunications, external connections to the internet, and internal infrastructure inside and among buildings. To receive most types of funding from E-rate and other federal programs, school districts and state education agencies must have technology plans. Key definitions, required plan components, approval information, and resources for technology planning are published on the E-rate website.

U.S. Department of Education's National Technology Plan
http://tech.ed.gov/netp
Reading existing planning documents is a necessary prerequisite for constructing new plans. The U.S. national education plan sets forth a vision for how technology can support teaching and learning. American schools will want to consider this vision and aligning local efforts to national goals.

State and District Technology Plans
www2.ed.gov/programs/edtech/techstateplan.html
State Education Agencies (SEAs) usually have technology plans. Finding and reading those plans may also be instructive. The U.S. Department of Education (US-ED) main-tains a list of state technology plans, but you may want to check your SEA's website for more recent documents. Some SEAs no longer have a separate technology plan but integrate technology-related goals into their agency plans. Reading your organization's technology plan or studying technology-related components in the organization's stra-tegic plan is a recommended leadership strategy. You might also consider reading other districts' technology plans for points of comparison.

National Center for Technology Planning
www.nctp.com
The National Center for Technology Planning is a comprehensive website founded in 1992 by Larry Anderson. The site contains helpful and relevant information, including free guidebooks for planning.

Technology Leadership Awards/Site Visits
www.iste.org/lead/awards
Learning from other technology leaders may enhance your own leadership practices. ISTE presents an Outstanding Leader Award and a Public Policy Advocate Award.

The National School Board Association (NSBA) also hosts site visits to exemplary school districts and recognizes 20 educational technology leaders to watch each year.

http://nsba.org/services/technology-leadership-network/education-technology-site-visits
www.nsba.org/services/technology-leadership-network/recognition-programs/20-watch

ISTE Advocacy Resources
www.iste.org/advocacy
ISTE has a comprehensive, free collection of resources to help educators advocate for educational technology. Members of ISTE's Advocacy Network receive emails with advocacy news, timely legislative updates, and action alerts on digital learning policy developments. The Voices Carry blog also provides up-to-date information on current legislative issues and public policies. The Advocacy Toolkit teaches educators how to take positive action to support educational technology programs. State-by-State profiles help educators connect with their state policy makers and state ISTE affiliates.

Concerns-Based Adoption Model
www.sedl.org/cbam
The Concerns-Based Adoption Model (CBAM) was developed by researchers at the University of Texas, Austin, and has been broadly used in education for more than three decades. This website, published by the Southwest Educational Development Laboratory (SEDL), provides a concise overview of the CBAM and directs readers to additional resources.

The Making Change Happen Game (often shortened to The Change Game)
www.thenetworkinc.org/games/leadership-series/mch
The Change Game is a simulation that helps players experience research-based characteristics of facilitating change in an organization. The simulation is available as a board game or as a computer simulation. Board games can be rented, and electronic versions can be purchased. Demos are available.

BOOKS

Books on Change

Technology coaches need to develop their own understandings of how change occurs, how to facilitate change, and how to support others through the change process. Of the many books on change, here are four that might helpful:

Dede, C., Honan, J. P., & Peters, L. C., Eds. (2005). *Scaling up success: Lessons learned from technology-based educational improvement.* San Francisco, CA: Wiley.

Fullan, M. (1993). *Change forces: Probing the depths of education reform.* Levittown, PA: Falmer Press, Taylor & Francis.

Fullan, M. (1999). *Change forces: The sequel.* Levittown. PA: RoutledgeFalmer, Taylor & Francis.

Rogers, E. (1995). *Diffusion of innovations.* (4th ed.). New York, NY: Free Press.

Books on Technology Leadership

Books specifically on technology leadership are somewhat rare; here are a few good ones:

Creighton, T. (2003). *The principal as technology leader.* Thousand Oaks, CA: Corwin.

Frazier, M. (2015). *The technology coordinator's handbook.* Eugene, OR: ISTE.

Schrum, L., & Levin, B. (2009). *Leading 21st century schools: Harnessing technology for engagement and achievement.* Thousand Oaks, CA: Corwin.

CHAPTER 2

Teaching, Learning, and Assessment

ISTE STANDARDS•C, STANDARD 2
Teaching, Learning, and Assessment

Technology coaches assist teachers in using technology effectively for assessing student learning, differentiating instruction, and providing rigorous, relevant, and engaging learning experiences for all students.

Helping others use technology effectively to support new ways of teaching, learning, and assessment stands at the heart of technology coaching. Thus, technology coaches must be skilled in curriculum and instruction as well as technology. In fact, technology coaches may be viewed as agents of instructional change who are also technology experts.

Because of the importance and complexity of what technology coaches must do to support curriculum and instruction, it is not surprising that Standard Two is supported by eight elements—more than any of the other ISTE Standards•C. The words "coach" and "model" appear in all eight elements, reinforcing the need for technology coaches to work closely with teachers in their classrooms to support instructional change. The eight elements related to teaching, learning, and assessment are:

- Content Standards and Student Technology Standards

- Research-Based Learning Strategies

- Meaningful and Relevant Learning

- Creativity, Higher-Order Thinking, and Mental Habits of Mind

- Differentiation

- Instructional Design Principles

- Assessment

- Data Analysis

Content Standards and Student Technology Standards

ISTE STANDARDS•C, 2a
Content Standards and Student Technology Standards

Technology coaches coach teachers in and model design and implementation of technology-enhanced learning experiences addressing student content and technology literacy standards.

For technology to impact student achievement in positive ways, classroom technology use must be tightly aligned to required content standards in math, science, social studies, language arts, and other disciplines. To help teachers create technology-supported, standards-based instruction, technology coaches must be able to locate and understand the content standards and model the use of high-quality digital resources that will help teachers implement the standards.

In addition to standards in core content areas, technology coaches must help teachers address important technology literacy standards in the classroom. Technology literacy standards, such as ISTE Standards for Students (ISTE Standards • S), describe what students must know and be able to accomplish to prepare for digital age life, work, and citizenship. Many states and districts have developed a detailed scope and sequence of technology skills to be taught at each grade level. In some cases, technology literacy elements have been integrated into content standards, making it much easier for teachers to know what to teach and when—but these scenarios are unusual. Since technology standards are not yet emphasized and assessed in the same ways as content standards, technology coaches often help teachers take the first steps toward integrating digital literacy into their classroom instruction.

Research-Based Learning Strategies

ISTE STANDARDS•C, 2b
Research-Based Learning Strategies

Technology coaches coach teachers in and model design and implementation of technology-enhanced learning experiences using a variety of research-based, learner-centered instructional strategies and assessment tools to address the diverse needs and interests of all students.

While aligning technology use to content and technology standards is important, it may not be enough to fully maximize student learning. For technology to be most effective, the design and implementation of that technology must also align to research-based learning strategies. The professional literature on effective instruction is vast, but good technology coaches will be well versed in research-based instruction and apply that knowledge to help others.

While there are many research-based strategies, this element highlights the importance of implementing learner-centered instruction and addressing the diverse needs and interests of all students. While these characteristics are hallmarks of digital age learning as represented in the ISTE Standards for Students (ISTE Standards•S), they are not necessarily easy to implement. Teacher-directed, one-size-fits-all instruction still prevails in many classrooms.

Technology coaches help educators understand how technology can help transform traditional classrooms into interactive, student-centered learning environments that meet the diverse needs of digital age learners. Coaches introduce new tools to teachers and demonstrate how they can help students drive their own learning.

Meaningful and Relevant Learning

ISTE STANDARDS•C, 2c
Meaningful and Relevant Learning

Technology coaches coach teachers in and model engagement of students in local and global interdisciplinary units in which technology helps students assume professional roles, research real-world problems, collaborate with others, and produce products that are meaningful and useful to a wide audience.

Students are more likely to understand, retain, and transfer knowledge when they are engaged in learning activities that are meaningful and relevant. Technology can enable this type of learning by helping students connect to a wider variety of topics and ways to learn.

For example, productivity tools help students research topics of personal interest, solve real-world problems, and create original products. These technology-supported practices aid students in constructing their own knowledge and demonstrating their learning—often in ways similar to practicing professionals in related fields.

The internet enables students to access information and collaborate with others in new and extended ways. With modern information and communication technologies, students can connect with peers, experts, and mentors—no matter where they are located. The connected classroom affords students opportunities to publish their work for broader audiences and to participate in civic activities. In many cases, technology can help students make significant contributions, such as extending knowledge in a discipline or improving their local communities.

While schools often have adequate access to technologies to support relevant, meaningful learning, many are not fully utilizing available technologies to participate in these new curricular options. Technology coaches advance relevant and meaningful learning by introducing new ideas and helping teachers implement them.

Creativity, Higher-Order Thinking, and Mental Habits of Mind

ISTE STANDARDS•C, 2D
Creativity, Higher-Order Thinking, and Mental Habits of Mind

Technology coaches coach teachers in and model design and implementation of technology-enhanced learning experiences emphasizing creativity, higher-order thinking skills and processes, and mental habits of mind (e.g., critical thinking, metacognition, and self-regulation).

Life, work, and citizenship in the digital age require creativity, higher-order thinking, and other habits of mind that describe how expert learners perform when they do not know the answers to specific problems.

To live and thrive in higher education and a digital economy, students need these types of thinking skills, yet many classroom activities and assessments are still predominately focused on memorizing and understanding facts and concepts. Mirroring this pattern, most student technology use in schools is focused on lower-order cognitive skills. While foundational knowledge is important, students also need opportunities to engage in higher-order cognitive tasks and to use technology in ways that help them become better thinkers and producers of knowledge.

A major challenge for technology coaches is to help teachers understand how technologies can support creativity, critical thinking, and problem solving. This might involve introducing stand-alone or multiuser games and simulations that present challenging scenarios to students. Helping students use productivity tools that help them analyze data and/or create original products is another option. Mathematicians, scientists, engineers, writers, historians, musicians, business leaders, and other professionals use a wide range of technologies to help them do their work and collaborate with others. Demonstrating some of those tools in classrooms can help students engage in similar types of collaboration and knowledge production.

TECHNOLOGY COACHING CASE STUDY

Sneaking Robots into the Classroom

—Allison Lydon
Head of Information and Communications Technology (ICT)
THE MARY ERSKINE SCHOOL AND STEWART'S MELVILLE JUNIOR SCHOOL
EDINBURGH, SCOTLAND

ISTE STANDARDS•C, 2a. Coach teachers in and model design and implementation of technology-enhanced learning experiences addressing content standards and student technology standards.

ISTE STANDARDS•C, 2b. Coach teachers in and model design and implementation of technology-enhanced learning experiences using a variety of research-based, learner-centered instructional strategies and assessment tools to address the diverse needs and interests of all students.

ISTE STANDARDS•C, 2d. Coach teachers in and model design and implementation of technology-enhanced learning experiences emphasizing creativity, higher-order thinking skills and processes, and mental habits of mind (e.g., critical thinking, metacognition, and self-regulation).

Head of ICT Alison Lydon describes her strategies to integrate programmable robots into the preschool and primary curriculum as "slightly sneaky."

She first introduced the robots to small groups of children, who then badgered their teachers to use them in class. When teachers asked Lydon about the robots, she offered to model a lesson in their classrooms while teachers observed.

When she knew teachers were ready to implement the robots on their own, she gently "weaned" them. The teachers continued to invite her into their classrooms, but she would tell them, "Oh, I am busy that day, but you can do it yourself. You've seen me, and the children know how to use the bots!" Of course, she sometimes hovered, making sure she was available if teachers needed assistance.

Over a two-year period, Lydon increased the inventory of robots, and they are now a regular part of the curriculum in 22 classrooms. She has also created take-home "Bot Boxes" with more than 30 themed activities. Each student takes home a robot two times a semester and practices sequencing, math, and literacy skills with family members.

"We already had take-home story boxes with books, so I just decided to add in some robot activities. Over time, I kept creating more activities. I get an idea, and it is great fun to sit down on a Sunday afternoon and create them," says Lydon.

After 20 years of helping teachers integrate technology into the curriculum, Lydon offers this advice to beginning technology coaches: "There is always a way to hook everybody. You just have to figure out the right angle."

TECHNOLOGY COACHING CASE STUDY

Coaching from the Classroom

—Adam Taylor
Science Teacher
OVERTON HIGH SCHOOL
NASHVILLE, TENNESSEE

ISTE STANDARDS•C, 2a. Coach teachers in and model design and implementation of technology-enhanced learning experiences addressing content standards and student technology standards.

ISTE STANDARDS•C, 2b. Coach teachers in and model design and implementation of technology-enhanced learning experiences using a variety of research-based, learner-centered instructional strategies and assessment tools to address the diverse needs and interests of all students.

ISTE STANDARDS•C, 2c. Coach teachers in and model engagement of students in local and global interdisciplinary units in which technology helps students assume professional roles, research real-world problems, collaborate with others, and produce products that are meaningful and useful to a wide audience.

ISTE STANDARDS•C, 2d. Coach teachers in and model design and implementation of technology-enhanced learning experiences emphasizing creativity, higher-order thinking skills and processes, and mental habits of mind (e.g., critical thinking, metacognition, and self-regulation).

Full-time teacher Adam Taylor uses Twitter to bring real-world science into his high school curriculum and helps other teachers do the same.

Taylor began using Twitter by following practicing scientists who were posting on content related to his curriculum. Now, he assigns his students to follow selected scientists. The up-to-date information from scientists enriches classroom discussions and helps students improve their academic discourse—an important goal since over half of Taylor's students are English language learners.

Recently, Taylor has been arranging real-time chats with the scientists and using his online professional networks to invite other schools to join in. Sometimes the time barriers are an issue, but he and his students have connected with classrooms in Canada, several European countries, and Pakistan.

Students also use Twitter as a back channel during class lectures and presentations. Taylor believes this has supported student language acquisition: "When students don't understand a term, they ask a question and others in the classroom answer it. It's a way for students to help others learn, and everyone can actively respond to the ideas being discussed."

Taylor has shared what he is doing with other teachers in his school and district through informal conversations and more structured professional development opportunities. He has also shared his work with district leaders at the Metro Nashville Public Schools Principals' Retreat.

Outside his district, Taylor has presented at National Science Foundation GK–12 Conferences, the Tennessee Educator Technology Conference, the Tennessee Science Teacher Association Conference, regional TeachMeets, and ISTE's annual conference.

Taylor's well-received work gives other teachers concrete ideas of how they can use Web 2.0 tools to enhance teaching and learning. He explains, "I guess there is a sense of credibility because I am in the classroom doing it. I can model ideas and strategies that already work. If other teachers are interested, I am very willing to coach them. We all want to improve student learning."

Differentiation

ISTE STANDARDS•C, 2e

Differentiation

Technology coaches coach teachers in and model design and implementation of technology-enhanced learning experiences using differentiation, including adjusting content, process, product, and learning environment based upon student readiness levels, learning styles, interests, and personal goals.

Traditional models of classroom instruction center on whole-group instruction and the assumption that a single instructional approach can meet the needs of all learners. In contrast, differentiated models of instruction recognize that not all learners achieve academic goals in the same ways.

Differentiated instruction often involves implementing multiple strategies to meet students' unique readiness levels, learning styles, interests, and personal goals. To meet these different needs, teachers often have to modify (1) instructional materials and learning goals; (2) instructional activities; (3) artifacts that will provide evidence of student learning; and (4) the arrangement, routines, and culture of the classroom. These changeable dimensions of classroom instruction are frequently referred to as content, process, product, and the learning environment.

Implementing differentiation strategies to meet the needs of all students can seem overwhelming—especially when considering the number of students teachers serve each day. This challenge offers opportunities for technology coaches to model how technology can support, even enable, differentiation practices. For example, electronic information resources, tutorials, simulations, and games offer students a greater variety of instructional materials. Software features, such as adaptive testing and reporting functions, help teachers access student achievement information, identify learning needs, and modify instruction. With such a wide variety of productivity tools, students are able to represent their learning in different ways.

Instructional Design Principles

ISTE STANDARDS•C, 2f
Instructional Design Principles

Technology coaches coach teachers in and model incorporation of research-based best practices in instructional design when planning technology-enhanced learning experiences.

Broadly defined, instructional design is the process of planning face-to-face, blended, or online learning experiences. In some cases, the term is specifically used to describe the development of instructional materials, especially if they are technology based.

Based on this definition, technology coaches are instructional designers. They create model lessons and help teachers plan learning experiences for their students. They also make technology-based learning materials, assist teachers in making materials, and evaluate whether existing technology products are appropriate for instruction. Basic principles of instructional design include aligning the instructional objectives, learning activities, and evaluation methods.

Instructional design may be approached in many different ways. Different approaches are often called *models*; they can emerge from a wide variety of disciplines, including corporate training, university settings, or PK–12 education. Instructional designs can represent a wide variety of theoretical perspectives on teaching and learning. Given the emphasis on higher-order thinking and student-centered learning in the ISTE standards, technology coaches need a comprehensive understanding of constructivist learning theories and the instructional design models that support them.

Technology coaches also need to help teachers design instruction that adheres to the principles of Universal Design for Learning (UDL), a set of guidelines for optimizing educational experiences for all learners. Often associated with making instructional materials accessible to learners with disabilities, UDL actually benefits all learners. For example, providing instructional materials in both audio and print formats accommodates learners with limited hearing or sight, but it also supports students with auditory and visual learning styles and preferences.

Becoming well versed in instructional design is a comprehensive and multifaceted task. Over time, technology coaches should explore a wide range of learning theories, models, and techniques to expand their thinking. Having a strong knowledge of instructional design helps technology coaches make good decisions when they create learning experiences, evaluate products, and help other educators.

Assessment

ISTE STANDARDS•C, 2g
Assessment

Technology coaches coach teachers in and model effective use of technology tools and resources to continually assess student learning and technology literacy by applying a rich variety of formative and summative assessments aligned with content and student technology standards.

Technology holds great promise for enhancing current student assessment practices. With technology-supported assessments, teachers can assess students' learning more frequently and in a wider variety of ways. If teachers can create, administer, grade, and analyze assessments more easily, they have the time and means to gather more formative or intermediate feedback on students' performances. This type of assessment data can be used to inform instruction so that all learners can achieve mastery of subject matter before more summative or final assessments of learning are administered.

Technology coaches support teachers as they implement technology-supported assessment. For example, instructional software with adaptive features and enhanced monitoring and reporting components are becoming more common in schools. Student response systems and online tools are often available for electronically gathering student feedback. With a growing interest in lowering assessment costs and returning results more quickly, online testing is another emerging practice.

Technology coaches also help teachers use technology to assess students' work products, such as papers, presentations, projects, or portfolios, that do not necessarily have right and wrong answers. In these cases, technology coaches help teachers create checklists, response guides, and rubrics that can be used for students' self-reflection, peer responses, and instructor feedback. Technology offers many productivity tools, such as rubric makers, online forms, and collaborative writing tools, to support the creation and use of these types of assessments.

To successfully encourage positive, technology-supported assessment practices, technology coaches need to know more than just how to use a technology-related product. They also need an advanced knowledge of research-based assessment practices. To fully implement ISTE Standards•C, 2g, technology coaches must be able to help teachers with nontechnical issues, such as providing ongoing feedback, generating assessment items for a test, forming questions to gauge student understanding, and constructing effective rubrics.

Technology Coaching for Digital Age Teaching, Learning, and Assessment

What does digital age teaching, learning, and assessment look like? How does it differ from traditional instruction? The following chart represents how technology coaches strive to influence shifts from traditional to transformed instruction.

TRADITIONAL CLASSROOMS	Technology Coaching and Modeling	DIGITAL AGE CLASSROOMS
Focused on content standards		Focused on content and technology literacy standards
Technology literacy is not addressed or addressed in isolation from content standards.		Technology literacy instruction integrated with content-based learning activities
Learning activities follow a single, linear path.		Learning activities emerge/ evolve from the diverse interests and questions posed by students.
Instructional materials are primarily print-based.		A variety of media accommodates students' individual learning needs and preferences.
Direct instruction is the primary method used in the classroom.		Direct instruction is provided on an as-needed basis to help students to complete tasks or investigations.
Students memorize information through listening and taking notes.		Students discover and construct knowledge through a variety of learning activities.
Collaboration and interaction are limited to the local classroom and school.		Students learn from and teach others beyond their classroom and school.
Few connections are made to real-life applications of content.		Learning tasks are situated in real-world problems, questions, or situations.
Instruction addresses a single discipline and limited concepts.		Learning activities address multiple disciplines and concepts.
Classroom activities address lower-order cognitive tasks.		Classroom activities require students to engage in a full range of thinking skills, including evaluating and creating.
Technology is used to deliver content to students.		Students use technology to collaborate, communicate, create, contribute, and share.
Teachers generate assessment criteria.		Students often generate assessment criteria.
Teachers are sole assessors for student work.		Self-reflection, peer response, and coaching from mentors supplement teacher feedback.
Teachers are the primary audience for student work.		Students use technologies to create and publish products to a broad audience.
The primary purpose of student assessment data is to assign students' grades.		Achievement data is used to assign grades, assess student learning needs, and improve instruction.
Classroom teachers consider assessment data for their own students.		Educators collaborate to analyze student assessment data and improve educational programs.
Technology-supported assessment practices are limited.		Technology helps educators create, collect, report, and analyze student assessment data.

Free Student Response Tools for the Classroom

Many school systems purchase hand-held student response systems or subscribe to online student response tools. If you do not have access to either of these, try gathering student responses from any of these free online tools:

Exitticket. **http://exitticket.org**

Kahoot! **https://getkahoot.com**

Padlet. **https://padlet.com**

Poll Everywhere. **www.polleverywhere.com**

Quizlet. **https://quizlet.com**

Socrative. **www.socrative.com**

TodaysMeet. **https://todaysmeet.com**

Data Analysis

ISTE STANDARDS•C, 2h
Data Analysis

Technology coaches coach teachers in and model effective use of technology tools and resources to systematically collect and analyze student achievement data, interpret results, and communicate findings to improve instructional practice and maximize student learning.

Being a technology coach also means being a data analysis coach. Technology can greatly enhance and facilitate assessment of student learning. However, collecting assessment data is only the first step toward using data to improve instruction. In order for assessment data to inform instruction, it must be analyzed.

Technology can support data analysis in many ways, and technologies are rapidly expanding in this area. Technology allows educators to visualize, compare, and contrast data. Technology-proficient educators are able to work with large data sets, look for trends over time, and make projections.

In supporting data analysis, technology coaches are likely to work with administrators and teachers. Administrators most often work with school and district-level data, comparing local performance to state and national information. Departmental and grade level data teams also have data analysis and reporting responsibilities. With data systems increasingly available at the classroom level, teachers are expected to enter and utilize data for individualized, differentiated instruction.

To support these new, sometimes complex practices in schools, technology coaches must be able to help educators use analysis and reporting functions in software packages. As with all good technology coaching, this reaches far beyond demonstrating how to use software and hardware to teaching others strategies for data analysis. Coaches show educators how to decide what to analyze, how to interpret what the results mean, and how to apply the results to structure improved student learning.

TECHNOLOGY COACHING CASE STUDY

Assisting with Assessment

—Charmona Whitfield

Site-Based Technology Specialist
LANIER MIDDLE SCHOOL
FAIRFAX COUNTY PUBLIC SCHOOLS
FAIRFAX, VIRGINIA

ISTE STANDARDS•C, 2g. Coach teachers in and model effective use of technology tools and resources to continuously assess student learning and technology literacy by applying a rich variety of formative and summative assessments aligned with content and student technology standards.

ISTE STANDARDS•C, 2h. Coach teachers in and model effective use of technology tools and resources to systematically collect and analyze student achievement data, interpret results, and communicate findings to improve instructional practice and maximize student learning.

Tracking the performance of every learner is a critical challenge for digital age schools. As site-based technology specialist at Lanier Middle School, Charmona Whitfield knows that one of her main responsibilities is to help colleagues maximize the use of technology to meet the challenges of assessment.

The district provides several types of assessment software. For example, one tool allows educators to review and analyze end-of-year state curriculum exams. Another allows teachers to administer formative assessments throughout the year. With the results of formative measures, educators can monitor students' progress before they take state tests and make critical instructional decisions to improve students' performances.

According to Whitfield, she spends a significant amount of time helping educators find the information they need from complex data systems. Once Whitfield locates the data, she must help teachers analyze it and think about what actions they must take. Spreadsheets are a valuable tool in this process. Whitfield attends district-level training on the assessment systems and brings that information back to her school. She also experiments with the software and finds the easy ways to do complex tasks. Then, she models these processes in faculty meetings, trains people in one-to-one or small group settings, and distributes direction sheets with step-by-step instructions.

Whitfield believes that her school is making progress in data collection and analysis, but she knows there is much more to learn. Her long-range goals include helping the school engage in more formative assessment activities: "We are required to administer some benchmark exams, but the assessment system could also be used to capture quick snapshots on teacher-created assessments. I know we don't want to test students too much, but there is still untapped potential for these systems. We are constantly learning."

TABLE 2.1. Technology Coaching Rubric for Standard 2

Standard 2. Teaching, Learning, and Assessment

Technology coaches assist teachers in using technology effectively for assessing student learning, differentiating instruction, and providing rigorous, relevant, and engaging learning experiences for all students.

a. **Content Standards and Student Technology Standards.** Coach teachers in and model design and implementation of technology-enhanced learning experiences addressing student content and technology literacy standards

b. **Research-Based Learning Strategies.** Coach teachers in and model design and implementation of technology-enhanced learning experiences using a variety of research-based, learner-centered instructional strategies and assessment tools to address the diverse needs and interests of all students

c. **Meaningful and Relevant Learning.** Coach teachers in and model engagement of students in local and global interdisciplinary units in which technology helps students assume professional roles, research real-world problems, collaborate with others, and produce products that are meaningful and useful to a wide audience

d. **Creativity, Higher-Order Thinking, and Mental Habits of Mind.** Coach teachers in and model design and implementation of technology-enhanced learning experiences emphasizing creativity, higher-order thinking skills and processes, and mental habits of mind (e.g., critical thinking, metacognition, and self-regulation)

e. **Differentiation.** Coach teachers in and model design and implementation of technology-enhanced learning experiences using differentiation, including adjusting content, process, product, and learning environment based upon student readiness levels, learning styles, interests, and personal goals

f. **Instructional Design Principles.** Coach teachers in and model incorporation of research-based best practices in instructional design when planning technology-enhanced learning experiences

g. **Assessment.** Coach teacher in and model effective use of technology tools and resources to continually assess student learning and technology literacy by applying a rich variety of formative and summative assessments aligned with content and student technology standards

h. **Data Analysis.** Coach teachers in and model effective use of technology tools and resources to systematically collect and analyze student achievement data, interpret results, and communicate findings to improve instructional practice and maximize student learning.

Approaches	Meets	Exceeds
TECHNOLOGY COACHES: • identify technology literacy standards (ISTE Standards•S and any local/state student technology standards) that must be addressed in classroom instruction and develop strategies for integrating technology into content-area instruction. (2a) • identify principles of research-based instruction, including the importance of implementing learner-centered instruction, meeting the needs of diverse learners, differentiating instruction, providing students with meaningful relevant tasks, and promoting creativity/higher-order thinking/mental habits of mind. (2b–f)	TECHNOLOGY COACHES: • coach teachers in and model design and implementation of technology-enhanced learning experiences addressing student content and technology literacy standards. (2a) • coach teachers in and model design and implementation of technology-enhanced learning experiences using a variety of research-based, learner-centered instructional strategies and assessment tools to address the diverse needs and interests of all students. (2b) • coach teachers in and model engagement of students in local and global interdisciplinary units in which technology helps students assume professional roles, research real-world problems, collaborate with others, and produce products that are meaningful and useful to a wide audience. (2c) • coach teachers in and model design and implementation of technology-enhanced learning experiences emphasizing creativity, higher-order thinking skills and processes, and mental habits of mind (e.g., critical thinking, metacognition, and self-regulation). (2d)	TECHNOLOGY COACHES: • provide evidence that their coaching and/or modeling practices helped other educators increase or improve technology use to support effective teaching, learning, and assessment strategies. (2a–h) • provide evidence that their coaching and/or modeling practices related to the effective use of technology for teaching, learning, and assessment resulted in enhanced student learning. (2a–h) • produce technology-supported instructional, assessment, and/or data analysis resources that are used by educators beyond the local school. (2a–h)

Table continued on next page

Table continued from previous page

Approaches	Meets	Exceeds
TECHNOLOGY COACHES: • Identify ways that technology can support and enable research-based teaching, learning, and assessment strategies in the classroom. (2a–g) • identify principles of effective student assessment and data analysis. (2g,h) • identify ways that technology can support effective student assessment and data analysis in K–12 schools. (2g,h) • implement research-based teaching, learning, and assessment strategies in their own classrooms. (2a–h)	TECHNOLOGY COACHES: • coach teachers in and model design and implementation of technology-enhanced learning experiences using differentiation, including adjusting content, process, product, and learning environment based upon student readiness levels, learning styles, interests, and personal goals. (2e) • coach teachers in and model incorporation of research-based best practices in instructional design when planning technology-enhanced learning experiences. (2f) • coach teachers in and model effective use of technology tools and resources to continually assess student learning and technology literacy by applying a rich variety of formative and summative assessments aligned with content and student technology standards. (2g) • coach teachers in and model effective use of technology tools and resources to systematically collect and analyze student achievement data, interpret results, and communicate findings to improve instructional practice and maximize student learning. (2h)	

Exemplary Performances in Teaching, Learning, and Assessment

The ISTE Technology Coaching Rubric describes performances that approach, meet, and exceed expectations for ISTE Standards•C, Standard Two: Teaching, Learning, and Assessment. This section is designed to provide an explanation of the rubric as related to Standard Two and to provide more examples in each category.

Table 2.1 illustrates how coaches can have positive effects on teaching, learning, and assessment. Note the differences in performances among the approaches, meets, and exceeds levels.

RUBRIC SCENARIOS

To support classroom technology implementation successfully, technology coaches need advanced levels of expertise in curriculum, instruction, and assessment. For example, the approaches category of the ISTE Standards•C Rubric for Standard Two highlights the importance of knowing about content standards, technology standards, research-based instruction, technology integration, differentiation, and assessment. For the most part, these approaches performances focus on acquiring foundational knowledge rather than applying it—with one exception. Often, aspiring technology coaches will have applied expertise in their own classrooms, but will not yet have helped other educators implement technology effectively. Implementing technology to support teaching, learning, and assessment in their own practices is a promising prerequisite for successful technology coaching, but it does not fully meet the standards.

APPROACHES

The following scenarios are examples of technology coaching performances that would be best described as *approaching* expectations for teaching, learning, and assessment. Note how these performances are all linked to important topics in Standard Two, but they stop short of helping others implement technology in their classrooms.

Sarah is a high school English teacher who recently learned there are student technology literacy standards. She began to study the ISTE Standards for Students and has reflected on to what extent she is addressing these standards in her own classroom. She also searched her state and district curriculum websites to determine if there are other technology literacy standards she and her department teammates should be considering when they plan instruction.

Greg is a well-respected master teacher who has taught elementary school for 12 years. He has attended many workshops and read books on differentiation and meeting the needs of diverse learners. He also implements many differentiation strategies in his own classroom. He is exploring how technology-supported differentiation strategies can enhance his efforts to support diversity in his classroom.

Perry is exploring various instructional design models and learning theories in his master's degree program in instructional technology. This study has shown him the importance of engaging students in challenging learning activities where they create useful, meaningful products. As a capstone project, he is designing an online learning experience for his students to research, write, and publish stories of Civil War events that happened their area.

Camille is a full-time technology coach. Her district has just launched an initiative to promote creativity, higher-order thinking skills, and rigorous academic content for students. To support this initiative, she attends district workshops to learn more. She hopes what she learns will help her locate examples of technology-supported lessons that meet the district's expectations for rigor.

Frederick is a high school department chair who is concerned with the growing need to track and report student achievement data. When reviewing new textbook options, he asked the technology coach in his school to help him review the electronic software than accompanies each product. He also asked the technology coach to help him understand the features of good monitoring and reporting components so he can become more independent in evaluating products on his own.

MEETS

There is no doubt that meeting Standards•C, Standard Two requires a great deal of knowledge about technology, teaching, learning, and assessment. Yet, neither possessing foundational knowledge nor integrating technology into personal teaching practices is enough to meet the standard. As implied by the frequent use of the words "model" and "coach," meeting expectations for this standard requires helping others use technology to support effective teaching, learning, and assessment practices.

The following scenarios provide technology coaching examples that *meet* expectations related to teaching, learning, and assessment.

Jasper is a media specialist who noticed that not many teachers were addressing the district's technology literacy standards. To raise awareness, he hung posters of the standards in the hall and found video examples of classroom instruction that addressed both content and technology standards. At a faculty meeting, he explained the standards to teachers, directed them to the videos, and offered to help grade-level teams integrate technology standards into one of their existing units of study.

Samuel volunteered to pilot some technology integration ideas for an existing unit on testing water quality in order to help teachers on his team use technology more effectively. He taught his students to use spreadsheets to record data and make graphs showing results of the experiment. To help his colleagues implement these new practices, he videotaped himself teaching the unit and made step-by-step handouts for teaching spreadsheets. He shared the videos and handouts with his colleagues.

Arabella is a part-time technology coach who is always looking for ways to help teachers use technology for relevant, meaningful learning. She observed that one teacher was asking students to write about important people in their lives and share their stories in class. Praising the project, Arabella suggested increasing the audience for student work by submitting their stories to an international website celebrating the brave and unselfish acts of others. She also offered to help students create word processing documents that meet the website's submission criteria.

Keaton is a full-time technology coach who presented a two-hour workshop for teachers on several free, online assessment tools. In the workshop, Keaton assumed the role of the classroom teacher and asked participants to behave as students. As Keaton enacted classroom scenarios demonstrating how the tools could be used, teachers visualized how they might engage in technology-supported formative assessment in their own classrooms. Following the workshop, Keaton helped many teachers design activities that suited their classroom needs. When asked, he also modeled the use of the assessment tools in teachers' classrooms, co-taught lessons with teachers, and observed when teachers used the assessment tools on their own.

EXCEEDS

According to the ISTE Standards•C Rubric for Standard Two, there are several ways that technology coaches can exceed expectations in the areas of teaching, learning, and assessment. First, technology coaches can demonstrate that they have influenced positive changes in others' instructional practices. Second, they can link their efforts to improved student achievement. Third, they can show that materials they created to advance tech implementation are being used by teachers and coaches in other district schools.

The following scenarios provide technology coaching examples that *exceed* expectations related to teaching, learning, and assessment.

Sara is a middle school technology coach. Several years ago, her district adopted the ISTE Standards for Students and created more specific district technology standards for each grade level. At first, teachers were unaware of the standards or how to implement them, so Sara provided teachers with examples of how to infuse technology into their content-based lessons. Now, students at her school are systematically taught digital age skills in all their core academic classes. During this same period, scores for the eighth grade technology assessment show marked increases in students' technology proficiency.

Juliette is a teacher who regularly used technology in her classroom. When she joined the sixth grade team last fall, she suggested that they participate in an online project about energy conservation. Her colleagues agreed. Students collected data on their local school's energy use, analyzed data from their own and other schools, and made suggestions for decreasing energy use. Students also collaborated with other schools and scientists to understand and apply energy-saving techniques. Teachers, administrators, parents, and students learned from and enjoyed the experience. The teachers decided to make this online project part of their regular curriculum.

Sandy is a full-time technology coach assigned to two high schools. As part of her job, she has been helping departmental data teams learn how to enter, extract, and analyze data from the school's student information system. Through this collaboration, the teams have been able to identify students who are not meeting goals and develop targeted strategies for addressing each one's achievement gaps. Even though these data-informed instructional practices are new, several teams are have shared success stories of improved student achievement.

Michael, a media specialist, and a team of teachers from his school aligned their district's technology and content-area standards for grades K–2. Then they developed technology-rich unit plans and published their curriculum on the school's website. Other schools in their district have used and adapted many of their lessons. The district Technology Department funded the group to continue curriculum development for grades 3–5.

Discussion Questions for Teaching, Learning, and Assessment

1. How is technology currently used in your school, district, state, or region? How frequently do students use technology? What types of technologies do they use? For what purposes do they use technology?

2. How is technology being used in your school (additional information that applies to your district, state, or region may be added here and throughout this list where applicable) to support higher-order thinking and mental habits of mind associated with expert performance?

3. Has your school district and state created and/or adopted technology literacy standards? Are they formally assessed? Do teachers know about them? To what extent are the standards being implemented in classrooms?

4. How is technology being used in your school to support the needs and interests of diverse learners? To what extent do teachers understand and implement differentiation, personalization, and universal design for learning?

5. How is technology being used in your school to support formative and summative assessments of student learning? What other technology-supported assessment practices would be beneficial? Why?

Essential Conditions Connection—ISTE Essential Conditions and and ISTE Standards•C, Standard 2

When implementing Standard Two–Teaching, Learning, and Assessment, technology coaches are contributing to the following essential conditions:

- **Curriculum Framework**
- **Student-Centered Learning**

TABLE 2.2. ISTE Essential Conditions Related to ISTE Standards•C, 2

ISTE Essential Conditions	ISTE STANDARDS•C 2. Teaching, Learning, and Assessment
CURRICULUM FRAMEWORK Content standards and related digital curriculum resources align with and support digital age learning and work.	Content Standards & Student Technology Standards (ISTE STANDARDS•C, 2A) Technology coaches help teachers locate content and technology literacy standards and address them in classroom instruction. They share resources and strategies that help teachers integrate digital age skills into teaching and learning.
STUDENT-CENTERED LEARNING Planning, teaching, and assessment all center on the needs and abilities of students.	Research-Based Learning Strategies (ISTE STANDARDS•C, 2b) Meaningful and Relevant Learning (ISTE STANDARDS•C, 2c) Creativity, Higher-Order Thinking, and Mental Habits of Mind (ISTE STANDARDS•C, 2d) Differentiation (ISTE STANDARDS•C, 2e) Instructional Design Principles (ISTE STANDARDS•C, 2f) Assessment (ISTE STANDARDS•C, 2g) Data Analysis (ISTE STANDARDS•C, 2h) Technology coaches help teachers transform their classrooms into digital age learning environments that model research and best practices. This transformation requires both instructional and technology coaching. Technology offers great opportunities to support meaningful, relevant, and challenging learning. Technology can also aid in assessing student learning and meeting the needs of diverse learners.

6. Are you pleased with the answers to these questions? What changes would you like to see? What strategies might support these changes?

7. What challenges do teachers face as they try to integrate technology into teaching, learning, and assessment? How can technology coaches help teachers overcome these challenges?

Resources for Teaching, Learning, and Assessment

The following resources relate to ISTE Standards•C, Standard Two: Teaching, Learning, and Assessment. Aspiring and practicing technology coaches may find these resources useful as they help other educators implement technology effectively in their classrooms.

STUDENT TECHNOLOGY LITERACY STANDARDS AND RESOURCES

The ISTE Standards for Students (ISTE Standards•S) and the Framework for 21st Century Learning are two resources that describe digital learning goals. To view these resources, consult these websites:

www.iste.org/standards/ISTE-standards/standards-for-students

www.p21.org/our-work/p21-framework

Two other information literacy frameworks are frequently used in schools, especially by language arts teachers and library media specialists. The Big Six is a process using a six-stage model to guide students through problem solving and decision making. *Standards for the 21st Century Learner* is a pamphlet published by the American Association of School Librarians. To view these resources, go to these websites:

http://big6.com

www.ala.org/aasl/standards-guidelines/learning-standards

Technology coaches should determine if their state or school district has technology standards for students. These standards usually contain a more detailed scope and sequence of knowledge and skills than those written for students throughout the United States. Arizona's and Maryland's state student tech standards are posted on these websites:

www.azed.gov/standards-practices/academic-standards/2009-technology-standard

www.marylandpublicschools.org/MSDe/programs/technology/techstds/index.html

INSTRUCTIONAL APPROACHES FOR STUDENT-CENTERED LEARNING

Many popular instructional approaches have emerged from constructivist learning theories and research on student engagement and critical thinking, including problem-based learning, project-based learning, inquiry-based learning, reality-based learning, service learning, and the maker movement.

For a comprehensive overview of how to design technology-supported, project-based learning and maker projects, the following books and websites provide concise and practical overviews:

Boss, S., & Krauss, J. (2014). *Reinventing project-based learning: Your field guide to real-world projects in the digital age* (2nd ed.). Eugene, OR: ISTE.

Hamilton, B. (2015). *Integrating technology in the classroom: Tools to meet the needs of every student*. Eugene, OR: ISTE.

Martinez, S., & Stegar, G. (2013). *Invent to learn: Making, tinkering, and engineering in the classroom*. Torrance, CA: Constructing Modern Knowledge Press.

November, A. (2013). *Who owns the learning? Preparing students for success in the digital age*. Bloomington, IN: Solution Tree Press.

For additional resources on implementing student-centered instructional approaches, see these websites:

Classroom 2.0, **www.classroom20.com**

Buck Institute for Education, **http://bie.org**

The Academy of Inquiry Based Learning, **www.inquirybasedlearning.org**

National Youth Leadership Council's K–12 Service-Learning Standards for Quality Practice, **http://nylc.org/standardsMaker Education Initiative, http://makered.org**

Sylvia's Super-Awesome Maker Show, **http://sylviashow.com**

Make: magazine, **http://makezine.com**

TECHNOLOGY INTEGRATION FRAMEWORKS

Several technology integration frameworks address student-centered learning, higher-order thinking, and authentic/meaningful tasks. These frameworks help technology coaches identify characteristics of higher-level technology implementation. When coaches find missing components in teachers' implementation of technology, they can help them strengthen these areas. Sharing these frameworks with teachers is often helpful. As a start, consider reviewing the following resources:

An overview of the Levels of Teaching Innovation (LoTi) framework can be found at **www.loticonnection.com** Chris Moersch, the creator of LoTi, has also published a book on digital-age best practices:

Moersch, C. M. (2013). *Improving achievement with digital age best practices*. (2013). Thousand Oaks, CA: Corwin.

Jan Herrington and collaborators have created the *Authentic Learning Model and Authenticity Matrix*, which can be accessed on their website. Though their work is slanted toward online learning and higher education, it is useful for face-to-face classrooms and K–12 settings. The home page for the authentic learning project can be found at **http://authenticlearning.info/AuthenticLearning/Home.html**; a list of books and online materials can be found at **http://authenticlearning.info/AuthenticLearning/Books.html.**

Ruben Puentedura has developed the SAMR model, which describes four levels of technology integration. SAMR-related articles and presentations can be found on Puentedura's weblog (**www.hippasus.com/rrpweblog**). Many other useful explanations of SAMR are available on the internet.

The Technology Integration Matrix (TIM) framework was developed by the Florida Center for Instructional Technology, College of Education, University of South Florida. This matrix and supporting resources, including videos of classroom practice, are available on the center's website (**http://fcit.usf.edu/matrix**).

THEORY AND RESEARCH ON STUDENT LEARNING

For an introduction to theory and research on instruction, consider reviewing one or more of the following books or reports:

Bransford, J., Brown, A., & Cocking, R. (Eds.). (1999). *How people learn: Brain, mind, experience, and school.* Washington DC: National Academy Press.

This book, sponsored by the National Research Council, provides an excellent, accessible overview of how people learn. The book was written with K–12 practitioners in mind. Although the book is older, texts on learning theory do not expire as quickly as some other topics.

Meyer, R. E., & Alexander, P. A. (Eds.). (2011). *Handbook of research on learning and instruction*. New York: Routledge.

This book is frequently used in graduate education programs to offer candidates an overview of theory and research related to classroom instruction and student learning. The content is somewhat challenging, and the book is expensive, but it should be available through libraries. It is a good resource for those who want an academic overview on a broad range of topics.

Roblyer, M. D. (2016). *Integrating educational technology into teaching* (7th ed.). Boston: Pearson.

In Chapter Two, the author summarizes several major theoretical influences on education and connects these theories to different technology integration practices. While Chapter Two directly addresses learning theory, the author continues the theme throughout other chapters. Though this book is often used as a university textbook, its content is accessible and practical. It is an excellent resource that surveys the different types of technologies available for K–12 classrooms.

U.S. Department of Education, Office of Educational Technology. (June 30, 2014). *Learning Technology Effectiveness*. Washington, DC: U.S. Department of Education, Office of Educational Technology.

This report is available at **http://tech.ed.gov/learning-technology-effectiveness**. This 17-page, readable report synthesizes major research trends related to technology and learning.

The Marzano Research website (**www.marzanoresearch.com**) contains a collection of resources for effective instruction and student engagement.

INSTRUCTIONAL DESIGN RESOURCES

These websites provide lists and/or overviews of many instructional design resources:

http://carbon.ucdenver.edu/~mryder/itc/idmodels.html

www.instructionaldesign.org www.instructionaldesigncentral.com

Among the most commonly referenced instructional design approaches are the Dick & Cary model, the ADDIE approach, and Gagne's Nine Steps to Instruction. Grant Wiggins and Jay McTighe's book *Understanding by Design* is also popular in standards-driven, K–12 educational settings. These models describe processes to guide the development of learning experiences and are general enough to accommodate various theoretical perspectives on teaching, learning, and assessment. Information on all of these approaches can be found online, but the following books provide in-depth information:

Branch, R. (2009). *Instructional Design: The ADDIE Approach*. New York: Springer.

Dick, W., & Cary, L. (2009). *The systematic design of instruction* (7th ed.). Upper Saddle River, NJ: Pearson.

Gagne, R. M., Wager, W. W., & Golas, K., & Keller, J. M. (2004). *Principles of Instructional Design* (5th ed.). Belmont, CA: Wadsworth Thomson.

Wiggins, G., & McTighe, J. (2009). *Understanding by Design* (Expanded 2nd ed.). Upper Saddle River, NJ: Pearson.

M. D. Roblyer's *Technology integration planning (TIP)* model of the instructional design process is tailored to integrating technology into K–12 instruction. This process is also flexible enough to accommodate various theoretical perspectives. See also

Roblyer, M. D. (2016). *Integrating educational technology into teaching* (7th ed.). Boston: Pearson.

The Center for Applied Special Technology (CAST) and the National Center on Universal Design for Learning are two organizations that provide comprehensive information, resources, and professional development on the Universal Design for Learning:

www.cast.org

www.udlcenter.org

CRITICAL THINKING FRAMEWORKS

Several frameworks describe critical thinking skills. These include Anderson & Krathwohl's Revision of Bloom's taxonomy, Marzano & Kendall's New Taxonomy of Educational Objectives, and Webb's Depth of Knowledge. Information on these frameworks is available from the following websites and books:

www.webbalign.org

www.marzanoresearch.com

Marzano, R., & Kendall, J. (2008). *Designing and assessing educational objectives.* Thousand Oaks, CA: Corwin.

Anderson, L., & Krathwohl, D. (2001). *A taxonomy for learning, teaching and assessing: A revision of Bloom's taxonomy of educational objectives.* New York, NY: Longman.

HABITS OF MIND

Arthur Costa and Bena Kallick's book Habits of Mind refers to 16 behaviors associated with higher-order thinking, problem-solving and creativity. The following websites provide an overview of these behaviors and information on how to encourage students to use them:

www.artcostacentre.com

www.instituteforhabitsofmind.com

http://habitsofmind.org

Online Objectives Builder

Arizona State University hosts Teach Online with its Objectives Builder designed by James Basore. This tool helps face-to-face and online teachers write learning goals at a variety of cognitive levels.

https://teachonline.asu.edu/objectives-builder

DIFFERENTIATION, PERSONALIZATION, AND INDIVIDUALIZATION

These different but related teaching approaches describe how education is moving from one-size-fits-all to customized instructional models, based on each student's learning needs, preferences, and interests. The following websites and books provide more detailed information about these models and how technology can support student-centered learning:

http://differentiationcentral.com

www.caroltomlinson.com

www.personalizelearning.com

Bray, B. A., & McClaskey, K. A. (2015). *Make learning personal: The who, what, WOW, where, and why.* Thousand Oaks, CA: Corwin.

Grant, P., & Basye, D. (2014). *Personalized learning: A guide for engaging students with technology.* Eugene, OR: ISTE.

Gregory, G. (2013). *Differentiated instructional strategies: Professional learning guide.* Thousand Oaks, CA: Corwin.

Tomlinson, C. A. (2014). *The differentiated classroom: Responding to the needs of all learners.* (2nd ed.). Alexandria, VA: Association for Supervision & Curriculum Development (ASCD).

ASSESSMENT AND DATA ANALYSIS

Helen Barrett specializes in helping educators understand and implement electronic portfolios. Many resources are listed on her website (www.electronicportfolios.org).

The following books on assessment offer helpful advice on assessment and data analysis:

Boudett, K. P., City, E., & Murnane, R. (2006). *Data wise: A step-by-step guide to using assessment results to improve teaching and learning.* Cambridge, MA: Harvard Education.

Love, N. B., Stiles, K. E., Mundry, S. E., & DiRanna, K. (2008). *The data coach's guide to improving learning for all students: Unleashing the power of collaborative inquiry.* Thousand Oaks, CA: Corwin.

O'Neal, C. (2012). *Data-driven decision making: A handbook for school leaders.* Eugene, OR: ISTE.

Tomlinson, C. A., & Moon, T. R. (2014). *Assessment and student success in a differentiated classroom.* Alexandria, VA: ASCD.

CHAPTER 3

Digital Age Learning Environments

ISTE STANDARDS•C, STANDARD 3
Digital Age Learning Environments

Technology coaches create and support effective digital age learning environments to maximize the learning of all students.

Implementing new teaching, learning, and assessment practices requires educators to create, manage, and maintain new types of classroom learning environments. New technologies must be carefully chosen and matched to students' learning goals. Once the technology tools arrive in the classroom, they must be arranged and maintained in good working order. When teachers implement new technologies and instructional methods, they often need to devise new routines and classroom management strategies.

In many cases, technology-enabled communication, collaboration, and online learning opportunities are prompting educators, parents, and community members to revise current views of schools and classrooms.

As described in ISTE Standards•C, Standard 3, technology coaches play crucial roles in providing support for emerging digital age learning environments in the following seven areas:

- Classroom Management and Collaborative Learning

- Managing Digital Tools and Resources

- Online and Blended Learning

- Adaptive and Assistive Technology

- Basic Troubleshooting

- Selecting and Evaluating Digital Tools & Resources

- Communication and Collaboration

Classroom Management and Collaborative Learning

ISTE STANDARDS•C, 3a
Classroom Management and Collaborative Learning

Technology coaches model effective classroom management and collaborative learning strategies to maximize teacher and student use of digital tools and resources and access to technology-rich learning environments.

Teachers are usually well-equipped to manage teacher-led presentations, whole class discussions, and activities with predictable outcomes. Likewise, students typically know how to behave in these traditional educational settings. However, when teachers and students begin to venture into the types of teaching, learning, and assessment practices described in Chapter Two, the culture of the classroom changes dramatically. Students pursue many different topics and learning goals. They work individually or in small groups. New seating arrangements are made, and students are often more mobile in the classroom. Noise levels change.

As technology coaches encourage teachers to move toward these instructional practices, they also need to be prepared to help teachers manage the changing classroom environment. To accomplish this, technology coaches can borrow from existing classroom management resources and collaborative learning strategies, but they also must learn to extend and adapt these techniques to accommodate technology-rich learning environments. For example, the availability of information and communication technologies enables new forms of collaborative activities with peers and mentors located outside the classroom. As students engage in these new types of collaborations, technology coaches must help teachers stretch existing collaborative learning and classroom management principles or create new strategies appropriate for digital age learning environments.

Managing Digital Tools and Resources

ISTE STANDARDS•C, 3b
Managing Digital Tools and Resources

Technology coaches maintain and manage a variety of digital tools and resources for teacher and student use in technology-rich learning environments.

Placing technologies in schools creates new maintenance and management tasks. Printers need toner cartridges and paper. Labs and laptop carts must be scheduled. Computing devices must be turned on and off, charged, and stored. In 1:1 and bring-your-own-device (BYOD) environments, management tasks can grow exponentially. In these cases, students have their own personal computing devices, and many different types of technologies can be operating simultaneously in a single classroom.

When technologies are introduced to the classroom, new rules and norms must be developed to protect schools' investments and to keep equipment operable. To avoid being overwhelmed, teachers need support in their schools to manage the new digital tools and resources. To provide this support, technology coaches often find, develop, share, and implement ideas to maintain and manage technology-rich learning environments.

Online and Blended Learning

ISTE STANDARDS•C, 3c
Online and Blended Learning

Technology coaches coach teachers in and model use of online and blended learning, digital content, and collaborative learning networks to support and extend student learning as well as expand opportunities and choices for online professional development for teachers and administrators.

Education is truly in a period of exciting transition. In the past, online learning space was offered principally by a handful of state virtual schools, some pioneering districts, and a few for-profit companies. Course credit recovery and AP courses for high school students topped the list of priorities for online content. While a small percentage of students took advantage of these online learning options, mainstream educational environments traditionally remained face-to-face.

In recent years, online learning has become universally accepted and available. Now, nearly every teacher has access to resources needed to implement some form of online learning. Blended and fully online learning environments for students of all ages have grown exponentially, and experts predict the trend will continue. Teachers can begin by integrating online content into their classrooms, blending some online learning with their face-to-face instruction or developing entire units or courses online.

Online learning opens new doors to support formal and informal professional learning opportunities for educators, too. Participating in online professional learning is an effective way for educators to experience what is possible in online learning environments.

To support the shift toward more online learning, technology coaches must be able to model best practices in K–12 virtual learning and online professional development for educators. Technology coaches will help teachers and administrators make good choices about online learning options and help reinforce the need for engaging, student-centered learning experiences in these new environments.

TECHNOLOGY COACHING CASE STUDY

Building Capacity for Online Learning

—Catharine Reznicek
Education Technology Specialist
VENTURA COUNTY OFFICE OF EDUCATION
CAMARILLO, CALIFORNIA

ISTE STANDARDS•C, 3c. Coach teachers in and model use of online and blended learning, digital content, and collaborative learning networks to support and extend student learning as well as expand opportunities and choices for online professional development for teachers and administrators.

Catharine Reznicek works for a county-based education agency serving 21 school districts northeast of Los Angeles. Her primary responsibility is to provide technology-related professional learning on topics her clients need and want. Right now, one of the most popular topics is online learning.

According to Reznicek, teachers and administrators are very interested in building their schools' and districts' capacities to implement online and blended learning. This is a challenge that she welcomes. Earlier in her career, she coordinated distance learning programs at a community college, but now she sees the climate is ripe for more flexible, robust, and interactive online teaching models: "We aren't talking about large lecture halls where we can stream video. Now, everyone has mobile devices, and access to the internet is readily available. People can connect synchronously with ease, and learning management systems make asynchronous teaching so much easier. Teaching online is becoming convenient and powerful."

To support teachers in transitioning from face-to-face to online environments, she is using the Leading Edge Online and Blended Learning Curriculum, a certificate program developed by several government and not-for-profit agencies primarily located in California. Reznicek completed a train-the-trainer program and is now able to redeliver the eight-week, online, asynchronous course to teachers in her service region. The course is designed to require only from four to six hours a week to complete, but Reznicek believes it effectively addresses key topics essential to implementing online and blended learning. When teaching the course, Reznicek models good online instructional practices and coaches teachers individually as they begin to implement online learning in their classrooms.

For many participants, the course is their first experience as online learners, but Reznicek notes they all grow in particular ways: "To me, the biggest success of the course is that very good teachers enter the course, and they become better teachers."

Promoting the Power of Connected Classrooms

Even though a growing number of classrooms around the world are connected to the internet, many are not yet fully harnessing the power of networked learning. Technology coaches can often help teachers and students understand the full potential of digital age learning environments by introducing some online projects and student publishing sites.

Online projects and student publishing sites support students as they collaborate with peers and mentors beyond their schools. While participating in online projects, students can solve problems, collect original data, and submit their results. Student publishing sites allow students to publish their original work to broader audiences. Below are some examples of what is possible in the connected classroom:

Journey North (www.journeynorth.org)
All Grades

Journey North is an online project that invites students to collect, submit, and analyze data on a variety of wildlife migration and other topics that change with the seasons. Through these experiences, students assume roles as scientists and learn standards connected to the inquiry process, the environment, seasonal changes, math, life cycles, and others. Math, language arts, and social science can also be integrated.

Go North Adventure Learning (www.polarhusky.com)
All Grades

Go North allows students to follow/interact with explorers traveling to Arctic regions. Students study science, geography, and culture and are able to communicate with researchers and other classrooms as they solve problems and engage in investigations.

Planting Science (www.plantingscience.org)
All Grades

Planting Science is a learning community where scientists provide online mentorship to student teams as they design and think through their own inquiry projects. Best projects or "Star Projects" receive awards.

Illinois Veterans and Community Classroom Project (http://ilvets.ltc.k12.il.us/ilvets)

The Illinois Veterans and Community Classroom Project captures the experiences of WWII, Korean War, Vietnam War, Gulf War, and other veterans and their families. Their project has produced 450 personal interviews—all filmed, edited, narrated, and uploaded by students. Most of the accounts have been archived by the U.S. Library of Congress and the Illinois State Library.

MY HERO Project (www.myhero.com)
All Grades

The MY HERO project is sponsored by a not-for-profit agency that invites students to share stories, images, and short films celebrating their heroes around the world. The site is translated into Spanish. The project has a Global Exchange component that fosters intercultural communication and understanding.

Project FeederWatch (http://feederwatch.org)

FeederWatch invites participants to count the types of birds they see at their feeders from November through early April and to submit their counts to Project FeederWatch. FeederWatch data help scientists track broadscale movements of winter bird populations and long-term trends in bird distribution and abundance.

Little Kids Rock (www.littlekidsrock.org)
All Grades

This music project is intended for students in economically challenged schools, but there are resources for all teachers on the website. The project started with one teacher in 1996 who was frustrated with the lack of funding for music education at his school. Now, Little Kids Rock is a not-for-profit foundation supported by many big-name artists. The foundation provides musical instruments to schools and guidance to music teachers and young artists. Students are encouraged to perform and share their music. There are many student videos on the Little Kids Rock YouTube channel.

Math-O-Vision (http://math-o-vision.com)
All Grades

Math-O-Vision is an annual contest where students can submit a four-minute video on math concepts and connections to real life. The first prize winner receives $3,000, and other cash prizes are awarded. Videos submitted are not allowed to be submitted to other contests the same year. The contest is sponsored by the Dartmouth College Math Department and the Neukom Institute for Computational Science. Previous winners are posted on the site.

Scholastic's Writing with Writers Project (http://teacher.scholastic.com/writewit/index.htm)
Elementary and Middle School

Students have access to authors, editors, and illustrators as they work on various types of writing projects. Students have the options to submit original work and to read other students' work. Teaching materials are provided for grades 1–2; 3–5; and 9–12. While high school materials are provided, the site looks and feels like a site for elementary and early middle school students.

MATHCOUNTS (www.mathcounts.org)
Middle School

MATHCOUNTS is a not-for-profit organization dedicated to improving middle school students' abilities to understand math. The foundation sponsors competitions, clubs, and a math video challenge. In the video challenge, four students create a video that teaches the solution to one of the problems from the *MATHCOUNTS School Handbook* and demonstrates the real-world application of the math concept used in the problem. Each member of the winning team receives a $1,000 scholarship.

The Jason Project (www.jason.org)
All Grades

The JASON Project connects students with great explorers and great events to inspire and motivate them to excel in science, technology, engineering, and math (STEM). The site embeds cutting-edge research from NASA, NOAA, the U.S. Department of Energy, the National Geographic Society, and other leading organizations. JASON students work side by side with practicing scientists and apply their knowledge to the real-world scenarios scientists face every day. The JASON Project was founded in 1989 by Robert D. Ballard, the oceanographer and explorer who discovered the shipwreck of the RMS *Titanic*.

Nature's Notebook Project (www.usanpn.org)
All Grades

Nature's Notebook is a project developed by the USA National Phenology Network. It involves scientists and volunteers who monitor the impact of climate change on a variety of plants and animals. In this project, students and teachers can participate in an existing project or start a new one.

Global Children's Art Gallery (www.naturalchild.org)
All Grades

The Global Children's Art Gallery, sponsored by the Natural Child Project, accepts submissions from children up to 12 years old. This site seeks to promotes a world where all children are treated with respect, understanding, and compassion.

ePals Projects and Global Classroom (www.epals.com/#!/info/about)
All Grades

ePals provides collaborative technologies for schools to connect in a protected, project-based learning network. Teachers can use ePals' website to find existing projects or as a tool to find partner classrooms and create their own projects.

ProjectsByJen (www.projectsbyjen.com)
Elementary

Created by educator Jennifer Wagner, this website houses online projects for students in grades PK–6. See the "projects" tab. This site is one of the few with instructional content and materials for students in the primary grades.

Online Projects for Kids from Vicki Blackwell's Internet Guide for Educators (www.vicki-blackwell.com/projects.html)
Elementary and Middle School

Vicki Blackwell has compiled a list of online projects for kids. Check her Blackwell's Best list (www.vickiblackwell.com/best.html) that notes some updated sites.

Center for Innovation in Engineering and Science Education (CIESE) Projects (www.ciese.org/materials/k12)

CIESE sponsors and designs innovative, interactive lessons and projects that promote problem-based learning, collaboration, higher order thinking skills, and critical analysis through the integration of science, technology, engineering, math, and other core subjects.

Class2Class Project Directory (http://mathforum.org/class2class)
All Grades

Class2Class a clearinghouse designed to facilitate students' and class participation in internet projects, including collaborative projects, data-collecting experiments, peer tutoring, and keypal exchanges. The projects must contain math, but also include other disciplines. The site has many elementary and some high school projects.

Connect All Schools (www.connectallschools.org)

Connect All Schools is a consortium of over 100 organizations interested linking U.S. schools with others around the world. The website highlights stories from classrooms that have been successful in leveraging the internet to support communication and collaboration with other schools.

Adaptive and Assistive Technology

ISTE STANDARDS•C, 3d

Adaptive and Assistive Technology

Technology coaches select, evaluate, and facilitate the use of adaptive and assistive technologies to support student learning.

According to the Individuals with Disabilities Education Improvement Act (IDEA) of 2004, an assistive technology device is defined as:

> "any item, piece of equipment, or product system, whether acquired commercially off the shelf, modified, or customized, that is used to increase, maintain, or improve the functional capabilities of a child with disabilities. IDEA 2004 specifically excludes a medical device that is surgically implanted or the replacement of such a device."
> (Mittler, J., 2007)

Adaptive technology is usually used as a synonym for assistive technology, but some educators use this term to refer to a specific type or subset of assistive technology. A narrower definition of adaptive technologies would be devices that modify existing tools. For example, a magnifying device for a computer screen would be considered an adaptive technology.

Many school systems employ technology coaches who focus solely on adaptive and assistive technologies and on helping special education teachers and students to use these tools. A background in special education is especially helpful for these coaches, often called assistive technology specialists.

All technology coaches should have a general understanding of assistive and adaptive technologies and be able to identify, select, and evaluate the appropriate devices. They should also be able to help teachers, students, and parents learn to use the tools effectively to support learning.

TECHNOLOGY COACHING CASE STUDY

Assisting Teachers with Assistive Technology

—Christopher Bugaj
Assistive Technology Trainer
LOUNDOUN COUNTY PUBLIC SCHOOLS
ASHBURN, VIRGINIA

ISTE STANDARDS•C, 3d. Select, evaluate, and facilitate the use of adaptive and assistive technologies to support student learning.

Christopher Bugaj is passionate about assistive technologies because they create new learning options for students.

"Once upon a time, every classroom looked exactly the same, and every student did the same activities in the same way, but this mode of learning is crumbling. Now, we look at individual learners and how they learn best. It's okay if one student writes a report while another creates a comic strip," Bugaj explains.

Bugaj helps teachers at two high schools, two middle schools, and eight elementary schools explore the best assistive technology options for their students.

He sends out an assistive technology strategy-of-the-day email. He also helps teachers on a case-by-case basis when they are striving to meet students' individual learning needs.

Sometimes teachers explain students' learning issues in an email, and Bugaj is able to offer suggestions in writing. In other cases, Bugaj schedules classroom visits to understand the issue or to assist the teacher in implementing a technology-based solution.

For example, many students are able to verbalize thoughts, but they have difficulty writing them. For these students, Bugaj might recommend speech-to-text software or recording an audio file in place of a written report. If teachers need support in learning a new technology to help their students, Bugaj will help them become comfortable with the product.

Bugaj has coauthored a book on assistive technologies. He also maintains a website with assistive technology resources, conducts professional development workshops in other districts, and produces regular podcasts on assistive technology topics. In his coaching activities, he is well-known for integrating humor into his teaching and modeling differentiation strategies for teachers to use with their students.

"Modeling best practices is key when trying to support change—and having fun never hurts," Bugaj notes. "Even if people are laughing at me, it's okay. They walk away with a strategy that might help their students learn!"

Basic Troubleshooting

ISTE STANDARDS•C, 3e
Basic Troubleshooting

Technology coaches troubleshoot basic software, hardware, and connectivity problems common in digital learning environments.

Technology coaches are not technicians. The focus of their work is instructional, not on fixing broken equipment. However, in their daily work with teachers and students, they will encounter technical issues, resolve them, and help others learn how to respond to problems when they occur again. Their technical expertise and problem solving ability are factors that set them apart from other types of educational coaches.

According to ISTE Standards • C 3e, technology coaches need to have knowledge and skills in the areas of basic software, hardware, and connectivity. Much of this knowledge is specific to their work settings. Gaining expertise in troubleshooting requires experience working with the hardware and software purchased by the school district and knowing the local infrastructure. District technical staff, print and web-based technical manuals, and online help forums are other key sources of information.

Selecting and Evaluating Digital Tools & Resources

ISTE STANDARDS•C, 3f

Selecting and Evaluating Digital Tools & Resources

Technology coaches collaborate with teachers and administrators to select and evaluate digital tools and resources that enhance teaching and learning and are compatible with the school technology infrastructure.

Digital age learning environments require a wide range of technologies—software, hardware, peripherals, and web-based resources. Technology coaches play a key role in equipping classrooms with tools and resources that enhance teaching and learning.

Technology coaches constantly scan for new technologies, ranging from free, web-based resources to software and hardware requiring substantial purchases. Technology coaches are also keen evaluators of these resources. They select tools that support student acquisition of required learning standards and promote the student-centered, authentic learning principles described in ISTE Standards•C, Standard 2. They ensure that the technologies are compatible with each school's infrastructure. Since technology coaches will also support the implementation of the technology with teachers and students, coaches weigh the tool's ease of use compared with its potential benefits. While technology coaches don't always make the final decision on large-scale purchases, they use this evaluation process to find and suggest high-quality tools for some or all classrooms for which they are responsible. When they find a tool worthy of adding to classrooms' environments, they show it to teachers, principals, and technology directors, hoping that they will adopt and purchase them.

In other situations, teachers, technology directors, or companies ask technology coaches to review products and provide feedback. Sometimes technology coaches are asked to lead and demonstrate classroom pilots of a tool before final purchasing decisions are made. In any scenario, technology coaches' proximity to practice makes them valuable assets in selecting and evaluating digital tools and resources.

Communication and Collaboration

ISTE STANDARDS•C, 3g

Communication and Collaboration

Technology coaches use digital communication and collaboration tools to communicate locally and globally with students, parents, peers, and the larger community.

High-speed internet access and new digital communication and collaboration tools have the potential to change learning environments. Students can learn together with students around the world, connect with community members, and work with professionals who would be unavailable to them without technology. Educators can use digital tools to collaborate with their peers and bolster families' engagement in students' education.

However, adopting these technologies and changing long-standing communication practices in schools takes time. Even though schools are connected, educators need help to learn what they can accomplish with new tools. Technology coaches provide this support by using communication and collaboration technologies for a variety of purposes. For example, they frequently create and maintain school websites to connect with parents and

TABLE 3.1. Technology Coaching Rubric for Standard 3

Standard 3. Digital Age Learning Environments.
Technology coaches create and support effective digital age learning environments to maximize the learning of all students.

a. **Classroom Management and Collaborative Learning.** Model effective classroom management and collaborative learning strategies to maximize teacher and student use of digital tools and resources and access to technology-rich learning environments.

b. **Managing Digital Tools and Resources.** Maintain and manage a variety of digital tools and resources for teacher and student use in technology-rich learning environments.

c. **Online and Blended Learning.** Coach teachers in and model use of online and blended learning, digital content, and collaborative learning networks to support and extend student learning, as well as expand opportunities and choices for online professional development for teachers and administrators.

d. **Adaptive and Assistive Technology.** Select, evaluate, and facilitate the use of adaptive and assistive technologies to support student learning.

e. **Basic Troubleshooting.** Troubleshoot basic software, hardware, and connectivity problems common in digital learning environments.

f. **Selecting and Evaluating Digital Tools and Resources.** Collaborate with teachers and administrators to select and evaluate digital tools and resources that enhance teaching and learning and are compatible with the school's technology infrastructure.

g. **Communication and Collaboration.** Use digital communication and collaboration tools to communicate locally and globally with students, parents, peers, and the larger community.

Approaches	Meets	Exceeds
TECHNOLOGY COACHES:	TECHNOLOGY COACHES:	TECHNOLOGY COACHES:
• identify strategies for effective classroom management and collaborative learning strategies to maximize teacher and student use of digital tools and resources and access to technology-rich learning environments. (3a) • maintain and manage a variety of digital tools and resources in their own classrooms. (3b) • identify research-based strategies for using online and blended learning, digital content, and collaborative learning networks to support and extend student learning as well as expand opportunities and choices for online professional development for teachers and administrators. (3c) • experiment with online and blended learning, digital content, and collaborative learning networks to support and extend student learning in their own classrooms. (3c) • identify the types of adaptive and assistive technologies to support student learning. (3d)	• model effective classroom management and collaborative learning strategies to maximize teacher and student use of digital tools and resources and provide access to technology-rich learning environments. (3a) • maintain and manage a variety of digital tools and resources for teacher and student use in technology-rich learning environments. (3b) • coach teachers in and model use of online and blended learning, digital content, and collaborative learning networks to support and extend student learning, as well as expand opportunities and choices for online professional development for teachers and administrators. (3c) • select, evaluate, and facilitate the use of adaptive and assistive technologies to support student learning. (3d) • troubleshoot basic software, hardware, and connectivity problems common in digital learning environments. (3e)	• model efforts that have improved other teachers' abilities to manage technology-rich learning environments and/or implement online and blended learning in their classrooms. (3a–c) • provide evidence that their maintenance, management, troubleshooting, selection, and evaluation activities have resulted in increased student and educator access to technologies. (3b, 3d–f) • produce resources related to improving digital age learning. (3a–g)

Table continued on next page

Table continued from previous page

Approaches	Meets	Exceeds
TECHNOLOGY COACHES: • identify principles of basic trouble-shooting for software, hardware, and connectivity problems common in digital learning environments. (3e) • identify strategies and processes for selecting and evaluating digital tools and resources that enhance teaching and learning and are compatible with the school technology infrastructure. (3f) • identify digital communication and collaboration tools useful for communicating locally and globally with students, parents, peers, and the larger community. (3g)	**TECHNOLOGY COACHES:** • collaborate with teachers and administrators to select and evaluate digital tools and resources that enhance teaching and learning and are compatible with the school's technology infrastructure. (3f) • use digital communication and collaboration tools to communicate locally and globally with students, parents, peers, and the larger community. (3g)	

community members, set up video conferencing for teachers and administrators, and suggest online projects that bring new dimensions to classroom learning.

The types of communication and collaboration technologies that are available to schools are constantly changing. Mobile computing and new applications (apps) provide even more opportunities for interaction. By introducing and using these new tools, technology coaches help transform traditional classrooms into digital age learning environments that are meaningfully connected to local and global communities.

TECHNOLOGY COACHING CASE STUDY

Selecting the Right Tools for Science Inquiry

—María Fernanda Veloz Galarza

Technology Facilitator
COLEGIO MENOR SAN FRANCISCO DE QUITO
QUITO, PICHINCHA, ECUADOR

ISTE STANDARDS•C, 3f. Collaborate with teachers and administrators to select and evaluate digital tools and resources that enhance teaching and learning and are compatible with the school technology infrastructure.

ISTE STANDARDS•C, 3g. Use digital communication and collaboration tools to communicate locally and globally with students, parents, peers, and the larger community.

María Fernanda Veloz Galarza is the full-time technology facilitator at Colegio Menor, a private school serving more than 1,500 students in Quito, Ecuador.

As technology facilitator, she tests, evaluates, and selects appropriate technologies to support student learning. One of her first tasks was to recommend how teachers could use technology to address core content and technology literacy standards outlined in the school's strategic plan.

Galarza also helps teachers select technologies to enrich their lessons. For example, each year, eighth graders go on a problem-solving academic field trip to the Galapagos Islands. In 2014 the students studied and offered solutions regarding the overpopulation of goats on the island. To enhance the experience and to address required technology literacy standards, the teacher sponsoring the trip asked Galarza to help her find technologies that would help student gather, analyze, and report data. Galarza surveyed technologies available at the school and looked for free online resources. She recommended the use of spreadsheets, charts, and graphs. She also suggested students use Glogster, Prezi, and PowerPoint as ways to enhance their presentations to the community and other schools via the internet.

Galarza acknowledges that the teacher had already designed a highly engaging learning experience, but technology motivated the students to analyze, synthesize, create, and share their knowledge in new and powerful ways. "When popular devices used by young people are included in the classroom, students are more motivated to work than if these technologies are not used. By using technology in our classes, we are directing students' motivation towards their potentially undiscovered passions of life. Hopefully it will spark their interest to learn not to obtain a grade but for the sake of learning!" commented Galarza.

Performance in Teaching, Learning, and Assessment

The ISTE Technology Coaching Rubric describes performances that approach, meet, and exceed expectations for ISTE Standards•C, Three: Digital Age Learning Environments. This section is designed to provide an explanation of the rubric as related to Standard Three and to provide more examples in each category.

Table 3.1 illustrates how coaches can have positive effects on digital age learning environments. Note the differences in performances among the approaches, meets, and exceeds levels.

APPROACHES
The following Rubric Scenarios offer examples of performances best described as the *approaches* level toward meeting the Teaching, Learning, and Assessment expectations for technology coaches:

Terrance is a full-time technology coach earning a master's degree in an instructional technology program. He wants to coach teachers toward technology-supported, project-based learning but feels that he needs more knowledge about collaborative learning and classroom management strategies. For a class project, he reads professional literature in this area and asks other technology-savvy educators how they manage digital age learning environments.

Harriet is a principal interested in encouraging more blended learning at her school but has not yet decided how to do this. To help her make decisions, she visits two other schools that have implemented Flipped Classrooms and Bring Your Own Devices. Through her visits, she learns what types of support structures would be necessary to launch similar initiatives at her school.

Penny is a full-time special education teacher who would like to become an assistive technology specialist. She can define assistive technologies, has used some assistive technologies in her classroom, and knows about some other common technologies that can support students with special learning needs. However, she would like to identify more types of assistive technologies and understand how they can be used. To increase her knowledge, she visits several assistive technology websites and learns about many more devices. She also learns how to search these websites to find beneficial tools.

Cesar is a teacher who has just been given two release periods per day to engage intechnology coaching. He feels very comfortable with the instructional portion of his job, but is taking a class on basic networking to develop his technical skills. He thinks this class will help him troubleshoot simple connectivity issues at his school.

Helen is a teacher who uses technology in her classroom. In the future, she wants to help select new software for her department. To prepare her for this task, she observes a current committee charged with finding resources in another content area. Through her observations, she learns how the committee defines its mission, researches possibilities, evaluates options, and recommends products for purchase.

Larry, a full-time technology coach, schedules one afternoon each week for reviewing digital tools that might be useful for supporting positive interaction among teachers, students, parents, peers, and the larger community. He focuses on tools and online learning opportunities that would promote global communication and collaboration.

MEETS

The following Rubric Scenarios offer examples of performances best described as the *meets* level toward meeting the Teaching, Learning, and Assessment expectations for technology coaches:

Kirsten is a kindergarten teacher piloting the use of tablet computing devices in the classroom. When she first tried using the tablets, students had trouble following directions. To eliminate this problem, she developed several classroom management ideas and shared these strategies with other teachers on her team.

Natalie is full-time technology coach. Teachers in the schools she supports have access to a learning management system (LMS) purchased by the district, but they haven't been using the software very much. To address this problem, Natalie offered a series of after-school work sessions for teachers. In these sessions, she provided examples of how the LMS can be used and gave hands-on support as teachers created blended learning experiences for their students.

Raleigh is a classroom teacher who uses text-to-speech software to help some reluctant writers in his classroom. When he shared how this assistive technology helped his students, other teachers became interested in using the software. Raleigh provided hands-on demonstrations to several of these colleagues and to students in other classes.

Jack is a part-time technology coordinator supporting a large elementary school. Since his school allows students to bring their own devices to school, students frequently need help connecting to the wireless network. To ease the troubleshooting burden on teachers, Jack developed connectivity information sheets for the most popular devices in the school. If students are having trouble, they can follow directions and solve their own problems. When teachers are implementing a new, technology-intensive project, Jack also likes to be in their classrooms to help troubleshoot any unforeseen problems that arise.

Lizzette is an academic coach for a school needing to improve student achievement in reading. Since the principal had funding to address this academic need, Lizzette recommended that they investigate reading software. The principal agreed. Lizzette developed a rubric for selecting high-quality products and worked with a team of teachers to choose the best options.

David is a full-time technology coach who wants to help teachers and students maximize the robust connectivity they have in their classrooms. He created a list of online projects, collaboration opportunities, and student publishing sites aligned with required learning standards and shared these resources with teachers, hoping that they would use them in their classrooms.

EXCEEDS

The following Rubric Scenarios offer examples of performances best described as the *exceeds* level toward meeting the Teaching, Learning, and Assessment expectations for technology coaches:

Gretchen is a middle school social studies teacher who used an online project in her classroom. When her grade-level team showed interest in the project, Gretchen coached them on how to participate. Now, all the team members implement the project with their students. The teachers believe the project has helped students engage with and understand the content more deeply. Several parents have provided stories of how the project has ignited their children's interest in history.

Norman is one of 20 technology coaches in a large school district. In a staff meeting, the technology director charged all the coaches with reducing the number of technology trouble tickets for their assigned schools. Norman studied past tickets from his schools, determined the most common requests for support, and implemented strategies to help students and teachers solve the simpler technical problems. Over the course of the school year, the technical support requests in his schools dropped by 30%. In hopes of achieving similar results, other technology coaches in district asked permission to use Norman's training materials in their schools.

Herman is a full-time technology coach who supports five schools in his district. Two years ago, only 10 teachers in these schools had classroom websites. Herman met with the principals of the five schools and showed them how classroom websites could support parent involvement and student learning beyond the school day. The principals agreed to ask their teachers to establish classroom websites over the next two years. Herman supported the effort by meeting with small groups of teachers. He showed them examples of effective class websites and taught them how to use Web 2.0 tools to create their own. He provided ongoing support as they created and updated their sites. He also trained a cadre of student webmasters who could help their teachers when Herman was unavailable. Now, all teachers in Herman's schools regularly maintain their own web pages. One teacher even received honorable mention in a national contest for exemplary classroom websites.

Barry is a professional development consultant for a state virtual school. He trains and supports educators who teach online classes for K–12 students across the state. Most of the teachers he supports have had little or no experience teaching online, but Barry helps them through the process. Last year, all the teachers Barry supported received

Essential Conditions Connection—ISTE Essential Conditions and ISTE Standards•C, Standard 3

When implementing Standard Three–Digital Age Learning Environments, technology coaches support the following essential conditions:

- **Technical Support**
- **Curriculum Framework**
- **Engaged Communities**

TABLE 3.1. ISTE Essential Conditions Related to ISTE Standards•C, 3

ISTE Essential Conditions	ISTE STANDARDS•C 3. Digital Age Learning Environments
TECHNICAL SUPPORT Educators and students have access to reliable assistance for maintaining, renewing, and using ICT and digital learning resources.	Classroom Management and Collaborative Learning (ISTE STANDARDS•C, 3a) Managing Digital Tools and Resources (ISTE STANDARDS•C, 3b) Online and Blended Learning (ISTE STANDARDS•C, 3c) Basic Troubleshooting (ISTE STANDARDS•C, 3e) As digital age learning environments evolve, technology coaches help teachers establish new routines, procedurses, and practices. They are especially active in fostering the transition from purely face-to-face learning to online and blended learning. Technology coaches also engage in basic troubleshooting and help teachers hone their troubleshooting skills, as well.
CURRICULUM FRAMEWORK Content standards and related digital curriculum resources align with and support digital age learning and work.	Adaptive and Assistive Technology (ISTE STANDARDS•C, 3d) Selecting and Evaluating Digital Tools and Resources (ISTE STANDARDS•C, 3f) Technology coaches carefully select technologies and digital curriculum resources that are aligned with content standards and support student-centered instruction. They also evaluate, select, and help others use adaptive technologies necessary for students to access the required curriculum.
ENGAGED COMMUNITIES Leaders and educators develop and maintain partnerships and collaboration within the community to support and fund the use of ICT and digital learning resources.	Communication and Collaboration (ISTE STANDARDS•C, 3g) Technology Coaches show how learning environments extend beyond the classroom. They select and model the use of communication and collaboration tools to connect students with peers, mentors, and community resources for learning. They also show how technologies can facilitate family engagement in students' education.

exemplary course evaluations. In an end of the year survey, they credited Barry with helping them become effective online teachers.

Josiah knew that students in his middle school classroom enjoyed creating real-world math problems for their peers to solve, but he thought it might be even more interesting if his students could share problems and solutions with other classrooms. To accomplish this, he created an online project called Go Figure. At first he invited teachers from his school district to participate, and eventually he gathered partners from across the world. Now more than 100 classrooms participate annually. Last year Josiah solicited corporate sponsors for the program. The sponsorship allows teachers to award prizes for the best problem and solution posted during each academic year.

Bobbie is a full-time technology coach who has helped teachers at her school implement flipped classrooms for over five years. At the beginning of the project, she kept a journal of her experiences. Several years ago, she transformed her journal into a website of flipped classroom tips for other educators to use. She also began using Twitter and other social media tools to interact with others who are flipping their classrooms. Now thousands of educators follow her work, and she is a frequent speaker at various educational events.

Discussion Questions for Digital Age Learning Environments

1. What are some of the best strategies you have found for managing collaborative learning environments?

2. What is the best way to arrange technologies in a school and why?

3. What strategies help teachers organize their technology-rich classrooms and keep technologies in good working order?

4. What are the pros and cons of Bring Your Own Device (BYOD) environments?

5. What issues must be addressed when planning and implementing a 1:1 environment?

6. At what age do students need their own computing devices to support learning?

7. What are some examples of how adaptive and assistive devices have helped students access the curriculum in ways that could not have been accomplished in any other way?

8. How "technical" should a technology coach be? How much should technical support be a part of their work?

9. How are technologies chosen in your district? How could teachers and students be more involved in selecting the technologies that are purchased? What are the pros and cons of teacher involvement in technology selection?

10. How is the connectivity in your school? How is that bandwidth being used for communication and collaboration to support learning? What else could be done to maximize the potential of the connected classroom?

Resources for Digital Age Learning Environments

CLASSROOM MANAGEMENT AND COLLABORATIVE LEARNING

Even though most technology coaches are experienced educators, everyone can always benefit from new classroom management and collaborative learning strategies. Since digital age classrooms are still evolving, many published resources are not technology specific. Technology coaches must take the principles of good management and apply them to new situations.

Websites

Cornell University, Center for Teaching Excellence: Collaborative Learning Resources
www.cte.cornell.edu/teaching-ideas/engaging-students/collaborative-learning.html

Iowa State University: Collaborative Learning Techniques
www.dso.iastate.edu/asc/supplemental/SIShowcaseCollaborative.pdf

Managing Technology: Tips from the Experts
www.educationworld.com/a_tech/tech/tech116.shtml

Te@chThought: 20 Collaborative Learning Tips and Strategies for Teachers
www.teachthought.com/learning/20-collaborative-learning-tips-and-strategies

We Are Teachers: Classroom Management
www.weareteachers.com/lessons-resources/classroom-management

Books

Burden, P. (2012). *Classroom management: Creating a successful K-12 learning community* (5th ed.). San Francisco, CA: Wiley.

Manning, M. L. (2012). *Classroom management: Models, applications, and cases* (3rd ed.). New York: Pearson.

Marzano, R., & Marzano, J. (2003). *Classroom management that works: Research-based strategies for every teacher.* Alexandria, VA: ASCD.

CLASSROOM MANAGEMENT TOOLS

Introducing technology into the classroom can create new management issues, but technology can also be used to facilitate good classroom management practices. These free or low-cost apps and websites provide some examples. ClassDojo is a positive reinforcement tool, and Watchkin allows for distraction-free YouTube searches and viewing. Too Noisy and Stopwatch help remind students of noise levels and time. For an overview of classroom management, several books and many websites with strategies are available.

ClassDojo, **www.classdojo.com**

Too Noisy, **http://toonoisyapp.com**

Stopwatch.com, **www.online-stopwatch.com**

Watchkin, **watchkin.com**

SUPPORTING 1:1, BYOD, AND MOBILE COMPUTING INITIATIVES

Schools are moving toward learning environments in which all students have their own computing devices. Below are some resources to help technology coaches understand and manage 1:1, Bring Your Own Device (BYOD), and mobile computing initiatives:

Websites

Common Sense Media's 1-to-1 Essentials Program
www.commonsensemedia.org/educators/1to1

Project RED, **www.projectred.org**

Educational Technology and Mobile Learning, **www.educatorstechnology.com**

Learning in Hand with Tony Vincent, **http://learninginhand.com**

INTEL's BYOD K–12 Blueprint, **www.k12blueprint.com/byod**

Kathy Shrock's Guide to iPads in the Classroom,
www.schrockguide.net/ipads-in-the-classroom.html

Books

Greaves, T., Hayes, J., Wilson, L., Gielniak, M., & Peterson, E. (2012). *Revolutionizing education through technology: The project RED roadmap for transformation.* Eugene, OR: ISTE.

Kolb, L. (2013). *Help your child learn with cell phones and web 2.0.* Eugene, OR: ISTE.

ONLINE AND BLENDED LEARNING

To support digital age learning environments, technology coaches need to keep pace with research, guidelines, and best practices in online and blended learning. The following websites contain important resources to help technology coaches be online learning leaders in their schools.

Websites

Christensen Institute for Disruptive Innovations, **www.christenseninstitute.org/education**

Flipped Learning Network, **www.flippedlearning.org**

International Association for K–12 Online Learning, **www.inacol.org**

Khan Academy, **www.khanacademy.org**

Multimedia Educational Resource for Learning and Online Teaching (MERLOT), **www.merlot.org**

Online Learning Consortium, **http://onlinelearningconsortium.org**

Quality Matters, **www.qualitymatters.org/grades-6-12**

Keeping Pace with K–12 Digital Learning, **www.kpk12.com/reports**

Research Clearinghouse for K–12 Blended & Online Learning, **http://k12onlineresearch.org**

Books

Bergmann, J., & Sams, A. (2012). *Flip your classroom.* Eugene, OR: ISTE.

Bergmann, J., & Sams, A. (2014). *Flipped learning: Gateway to student engagement.* Eugene, OR: ISTE.

Carlson, G., & Raphael R. (2015). *Let's get social: The educator's guide to edmodo.* Eugene, OR: ISTE.

Christensen, C. (2008). *Disrupting class: How disruptive innovations will change the way the world learns.* New York: McGraw Hill.

Christensen, C., & Staker, H. (2015). *Blended: Using disruptive innovations to improve school.* San Francisco: Jossey Bass.

Conrad, R., & Donaldson, J. A. (2011). *Engaging the online learner: Activities and resources for creative instruction.* San Francisco: Wiley.

Hirumi, A. (2014). *Grounded designs for online and hybrid learning series.* Eugene, OR: ISTE.

Smith, S., Chavez, A., & Seaman, G. (2014). *Teacher as architect: Instructional design and delivery for the modern teacher* (2nd ed.). Eugene, OR: ISTE.

Tucker, C. (2012). *Blended learning in grades 4-12.* Thousand Oaks, CA: Corwin.

FREE ONLINE LEARNING TOOLS

Many school districts provide teachers with a learning management system (LMS) to support online and blended learning experiences for students. If these more robust systems are not available, there are free options that allow teachers to create digital classrooms. These tools help teachers manage classroom resources and assignments.

Haiku Learning, **www.haikulearning.com**

Edmodo, **www.edmodo.com**

ASSISTIVE TECHNOLOGIES

Many resources are available to help technology coaches learn about, research, and select assistive technologies. These resources include assistive technology centers throughout the United States and indicators for high-quality assistive technologies. AbleData and the Tech Matrix allow users to search for available products. Many informative books on assistive technology can be great sources for new ideas.

Websites

AbleData: Tools & Technologies to Enhance Life, **www.abledata.com**

Center on Technology and Disability, **www.ctdinstitute.org**

RESNA Catalyst Project: Directory of State Assistive Technology Programs, **www.resnaprojects.org/allcontacts/statewidecontacts.html**

Quality Indicators for Assistive Technology (QIAT), **www.qiat.org**

TechMatrix, **http://techmatrix.org**

Books

Bugaj, C. (2010). *The practical (and fun) guide to assistive technology in public schools: Building or improving your district's at team.* Eugene, OR: ISTE.

Green, J. (2014). *Assistive technology in special education: Resources for education, intervention, and rehabilitation* (2nd ed.). Waco, TX: Prufrock Press.

Schad, L. (2014). *Bring your own learning: Transform instruction with any device.* Eugene, OR: ISTE.

TROUBLESHOOTING

Technology coaches learn to troubleshoot through technical manuals, online videos, discussion forums, calls to technical support, tinkering, and talking to peers. Listing all the resources that support troubleshooting would be impossible, but here are a few to consider. LearnFree has a tutorial on basic troubleshooting techniques, as well as many other resources. Microsoft and Apple tutorials and forums can help with operating system issues. Lynda.com and Atomic Learning are subscription services, and many schools use them.

Apple Tutorials, **www.apple.com/support/macbasics**

Apple Support Communities Atomic Learning, **www.atomiclearning.com**

LearnFree.org's Troubleshooting Techniques, **www.gcflearnfree.org/computerbasics/15**

Lynda.com, **www.lynda.com**

Windows Tutorials, **http://windows.microsoft.com/en-us/windows/tutorial**

Windows Eight Forums, **www.eightforums.com**

MULTIMEDIA AND GAMING IN THE CLASSROOM

Gaming and multimedia are two emerging elements in digital age learning environments. The following books provide some practical advice on how these elements can enrich learning:

Bass, W., Goodrich, C., & Lindskog, K. (2013). *From inspiration to red carpet.* Eugene, OR: ISTE.

Frazel, M. (2010). *Digital storytelling guide for educators.* Eugene, OR: ISTE.

Hearn, M., & Winner, M. (2013). *Teach math with the wii.* Eugene, OR: ISTE.

COMMUNICATION AND COLLABORATION

Though digital age schools are connected, many are not fully maximizing technology's teaching and learning opportunities. The following websites and books help technology coaches locate free or low-cost tools and enhance their creativity so that communication and collaboration with teachers lead to classroom practices:

Websites

Adam Bellow's eduTecher blog, **www.edutecher.net/index.php**

Apple Distinguished Educators' APPitic, **www.appitic.com**

Tammy's Technology Tips for Teachers, **http://tammyworcester.com**

Leslie Fisher's Blog and Gadgets presentations, **www.lesliefisher.com/resources/blog/**

Richard Byrne's Free Technology for Teachers, **www.freetech4teachers.com**

Books

Dembo, S., & Bellow, A. (2013). *Untangling the web: 20 tools to power up your teaching.* Thousand Oaks, CA: Corwin.

Parisi, L., & Crosby, B. (2012). *Making connections with blogging: Authentic learning for today's classrooms.* Eugene, OR: ISTE.

Richardson, W. (2010). *Blogs, wikis, podcasts, and other powerful web tools for classrooms* (3rd ed.). Thousand Oaks, CA: Corwin.

Solomon, G., & Schrum, L. (2014). *Web 2.0 how-to for educators* (2nd ed.). Eugene, OR: ISTE.

CHAPTER 4

Professional Development and Program Evaluation

ISTE STANDARDS•C, STANDARD 4
Professional Development and Program Evaluation

Technology coaches conduct needs assessments, develop technology-related professional learning programs, and evaluate their impacts on instructional practice and student learning.

Technology coaches are specialized professional development experts. Their core mission is to help other educators maximize the use of technology in schools. To pursue this mission, technology coaches need an advanced understanding of how teachers acquire new knowledge and skills. They also need to know which types of professional learning activities are most likely to help teachers improve their classroom practices. Technology coaches use their expertise to design, develop, and deliver high-quality professional development programs that help their colleagues learn *about* and learn *with* technology.

As stated in the standard, it is important that technology coaches create and implement *technology-rich* professional development programs. Technology coaches are leaders and should model the same types of digital age learning practices they hope to see in classrooms.

When technology coaches infuse technology into high-quality professional development efforts, teachers are able to experience digital age learning. These experiences help teachers fully understand technology's power to support learning and help them replicate similar types of activities with their students.

ISTE Standards•C, Standard Four contains three elements related to professional development that describe what technology coaches must know and be able to do to implement the following:

- Needs Assessments

- Professional Learning Programs

- Program Evaluation

Needs Assessments

ISTE STANDARDS•C, 4a
Needs Assessments

Technology coaches conduct needs assessments to inform the content and delivery of technology-related professional learning programs that result in a positive impact on student learning.

Needs assessments for professional learning programs consist of (1) collecting information on an organization's current professional learning programs, (2) identifying any gaps between the professional programs and the organization's goals for student learning, and (3) determining what actions are needed to bridge any gaps.

Good professional learning programs are responsive and informed. Conducting needs assessments is an important step in designing high-quality professional development programs. Needs assessments help technology coaches identify students' learning needs, based on the tech goals set for students, and teachers' current abilities to use technology in the classroom to meet those needs. Needs assessments also provide information on teachers' interests, personal learning goals, and individual learning styles.

By analyzing information gathered from needs assessments, technology coaches identify an overarching purpose and specific learning objectives for professional learning. Results of assessments also help technology coaches design and implement differentiation and individualized strategies for each teacher.

Needs assessments are usually associated with the initial stages of professional development planning, but good technology coaches also monitor the evolving needs of the communities they serve. Professional development strategies focused on goals for students' learning and targeted to relate to teachers' personal interests and learning goals are likely to be successful.

Needs assessments can be formal or informal, involved or simple. Technology coaches can engage in many different types of activities to gather information about each school's situation. Some of the more common options include the following:

- Analyzing student learning standards and student achievement data

- Observing classroom practices

- Gathering information from teachers, administrators, students, and/or their families through one-on-one conversations, interviews, focus groups, and/or surveys

- Examining artifacts, such as lesson plans, websites, student work, and technology products

TECHNOLOGY COACHING CASE STUDY

Modeling Technology Use and Classroom Management Techniques

—Kristina McBride, Information Technology Specialist
ITEACH CENTER, KENNESAW STATE UNIVERSITY
KENNESAW, GA

ISTE STANDARDS•C, 4a. Technology coaches conduct needs assessments to inform the content and delivery of technology-related professional learning programs that result in a positive impact on student learning.

ISTE STANDARDS•C, 4b. Technology coaches design, develop, and implement technology-rich professional learning programs that model principles of adult learning and promote digital age best practices in teaching, learning, and assessment.

K ristina McBride began her career as an elementary teacher. Since 2002, she has served as an instructional technology specialist at Kennesaw State University's iTeach Center. The iTeach Center provides technology-related consulting and professional development services to public and private schools, mostly in the Atlanta metro area.

McBride's work varies from day to day and can be demanding. Though most school districts and private schools have full-time technology coaches, tech directors and tech coaches often call the iTeach Center when something new or challenging comes along or when they need advice or extra help to complete a project.

One of McBride's recent projects was to support an iPad implementation at Sweet Apple Elementary School in Fulton County, GA. After receiving a generous donation of iPads and funds to support teachers' professional development, the school's principal contacted the iTeach Center. McBride, along with one of her colleagues, visited the school, listened to the teachers express their needs, and looked for iPad applications that would best support the teachers' learning goals. Next, McBride offered several lesson ideas to the teachers and let them choose what they would like to try.

The lesson ideas she suggested included using Show Me, Puppet Pals, and iMovie to help students create multimedia products demonstrating their learning. After teachers decided on a project, McBride scheduled time to model for teachers and students how to use the iPads in their classrooms. While the teachers assisted her, she taught students how to use the various iPad applications to complete their lessons, mindful of the school's desired learning goals at each grade level.

During this project, McBride noted that modeling good classroom management was just as critical as modeling technology use and effective instruction. "Once the students had the devices in their hands, they almost became too engaged! This is a nice problem to have, but I had to invent ways to regroup and get their attention again," laughed McBride.

McBride believes the best professional development is constructed and implemented with teachers in their own classrooms: "Having the opportunity to work with teachers and students is very powerful. I learn as much as the teachers do."

Professional Learning Programs

ISTE STANDARDS•C, 4b
Professional Learning Programs

Technology coaches design, develop, and implement technology-rich professional learning programs that model principles of adult learning and promote digital age best practices in teaching, learning, and assessment.

Professional learning programs are not one-time workshops or isolated instances of helping a teacher troubleshoot a technology. Programs are long-term, coordinated efforts designed to transform schools into digital age learning environments—and technology coaches are expected to *design, develop,* and *implement* them.

To make informed decisions about professional learning, technology coaches need a deep understanding of principles and practices for teaching adults, which is defined as andragogy (as distinguished from pedagogy, instructing children or adolescents). Technology coaches must understand that adults are already expert learners and want their existing professional knowledge and expertise to be valued. Typically, adults prefer self-directed learning and topics directly related to their work. Generally, adults learn better from actively constructing knowledge through solving problems or by producing practical products with peers.

Coaching is only one method of professional development, but it is an especially effective way for adults in the workforce to learn new concepts and skills. A successful coach must be an expert at developing personal relationships, giving individual attention, and modeling job-embedded learning. Excellent coaches also focus on their adult students' improved performances as the ultimate goal of professional learning. Emphasizing coaching in ISTE's Standards•C highlights these important principles of adult learning.

Aligning professional development to adult learning theory has a dual purpose. Not only will this alignment promote teacher learning, it will also model the kinds of learning environments teachers are expected to implement with their students. The principles of adult learning theory are similar to those of effective instruction for children and adolescents. High-quality professional development mirrors many characteristics of the active, challenging, student-centered environments described in the ISTE Standards for Students.

Professional Learning Standards

Learning Forward: The Professional Learning Association (formerly the National Staff Development Council, NSDC) is an organization dedicated to promoting high-quality professional development for educators. The organization publishes a list of seven standards or desirable characteristics for professional learning on its website:

Learning Communities: Professional learning that increases educator effectiveness and results for all students occurs within learning communities committed to continuous improvement, collective responsibility, and goal alignment.

Leadership: Professional learning that increases educator effectiveness and results for all students requires skillful leaders who develop capacity, advocate, and create support systems for professional learning.

Resources: Professional learning that increases educator effectiveness and results for all students requires prioritizing, monitoring, and coordinating resources for educator learning.

Data: Professional learning that increases educator effectiveness and results for all students uses a variety of sources and types of student, educator, and system data to plan, assess, and evaluate professional learning.

Learning Designs: Professional learning that increases educator effectiveness and results for all students integrates theories, research, and models of human learning to achieve its intended outcomes.

Implementation: Professional learning that increases educator effectiveness and results for all students applies research on change and sustains support for implementation of professional learning for long term change.

Outcomes: Professional learning that increases educator effectiveness and results for all students aligns its outcomes with educator performance and student curriculum standards.

(http://learningforward.org/standards)

Technology Coaching Strategies

What does it really mean to coach others? The following strategies describe some specific types of interactions and activities technology coaches use to help others learn.

Co-plan Lessons. Work with other teachers to plan future, technology-supported instruction in their classrooms.

Co-Teach Lessons. Teach lessons with other teachers to help them increase their comfort levels and/or to experiment with technology-supported instruction.

Model Lessons. Teach technology-supported learning experiences in a classroom so that others can observe, increase their comfort levels, and/or implement a similar lesson in the future.

Observe Lessons. Observe technology-supported learning experiences in a classroom facilitated by others.

Provide Feedback to Lessons. Provide praise, suggestions, and advice on technology-supported learning experiences implemented by others.

Plan Professional Development Events. Prepare for formal, technology-related professional development events, such as workshops, training, and presentations.

Facilitate Professional Development Events. Implement formal, technology-related professional development activities, such as workshops, training, and presentations.

Build Relationships. Interact with others for the purposes of building trust and mutual understanding.

Support Learning Communities. Provides the structure and resources needed to foster informal, technology-related learning opportunities, such as discussions, sharing experiences, and collaborative work.

Prepare Resources. Locate, adapt, or create materials to help educators use technology effectively for teaching, learning, assessment, and/or administration.

Share Resources. Disseminate materials that help educators use technology effectively for teaching, learning, assessment, and/or administration.

Develop Technology Literacy. Help others develop technical skills needed to implement technology-supported instruction.

Troubleshoot Technologies. Solve technical problems for others.

(Adapted from Technology Coaches for Instruction, Integration and Implementation, by Jana Craig-Hare, 2013.)

TECHNOLOGY COACHING CASE STUDY

Training Teachers to Enhance Best Practices

—Mike Wheadon

Information and Communications Technology (ICT) Integrator
SANTA SABINA COLLEGE
SYDNEY, NEW SOUTH WALES, AUSTRALIA

ISTE STANDARDS•C, 4b: Technology Coaches design, develop, and implement technology-rich professional learning programs that model principles of adult learning and promote digital age best practices in teaching, learning, and assessment.

Mike Wheadon supports K–6 teachers at Santa Sabina College in Sydney, Australia, where there is a strong, unique commitment to ongoing professional learning.

Each year teachers meet with the school's full-time Learning Guide to discuss what they need to learn in order to achieve schoolwide learning initiatives. Once teachers have set their personal learning goals for the year, the learning guide helps them identify strategies to reach those goals. Each teacher commits to spending 40 hours on professional development per year.

This is where Wheadon frequently joins the process. Since most teachers have a technology-related component listed in their goals, they ask Wheadon how he might help them achieve what they want to learn. Frequent strategies include individual or small group training sessions where teachers meet with Wheadon once or twice a month, but the strategies depend on individual learners' needs and their goals.

"At Santa Sabina, the teachers drive their learning," he explained. "I offer suggestions and support, but the decisions are ultimately theirs. They are responsible for meeting their goals, but what they choose and how they get there is totally up to them."

Wheadon also designs training for larger groups, but teachers' choices are still a critical component. Since Wheadon works closely with the staff, he is able to determine topics that may have a broad appeal. He designs workshops on those topics and posts information about them to a school registration site where teachers can pick classes that are most helpful to them.

"I like the way we do things," he commented. "The key is to stand back enough so as not to be imposing, but also to guide teachers gently so they can meet their goals. I find it best to offer suggestions and let them have the final say."

Program Evaluation

ISTE STANDARDS•C, 4c

Program Evaluation

Evaluate results of professional learning programs to determine their effectiveness on deepening teacher content knowledge, improving teacher pedagogical skills, and/or increasing student learning.

To determine the effectiveness of their efforts, technology coaches must be able to evaluate professional learning programs. Professional learning can be evaluated at many levels. Most technology coaches evaluate teachers' satisfaction with professional learning. Many coaches also monitor teachers' beliefs about using technology and their willingness or motivation to integrate technology into their classroom practices. Unfortunately, most program evaluation efforts end with these attitudinal measures and fail to address the higher-level outcomes that board members and stakeholders increasingly want to see.

ISTE Standards•C, 4c clearly challenges technology coaches to stretch toward higher-level evaluation goals. Technology coaches should be able to determine the extent to which their efforts are helping teachers (1) acquire new knowledge and skills, (2) change their classroom practices to make them more effective, and (3) increase student learning. Of course, these types of goals are much more difficult to measure—making this one of the more challenging elements for technology coaches to address. Becoming a good evaluator requires specific training and practice.

While challenging, this element is also extremely important. Technology coaches must be able to gather ongoing, formative evaluation data so that they can make critical improvements to their professional development programs. They must also be able to provide stakeholders with compelling, summative evaluation results, which are necessary in public and private schools to justify funding for professional learning, technology purchases, and technology staff.

TECHNOLOGY COACHING CASE STUDY

Implementing the ISTE Standards in Nigeria

—Olusola Dawodu

Managing Director/Technology Coordinator
SCHOOL WORKS ENTERPRISES
SURULERE, LAGOS, NIGERIA

ISTE STANDARDS•C, 4a. Conduct needs assessments to inform the content and delivery of technology-related professional learning programs that result in a positive impact on student learning.

ISTE STANDARDS•C, 4b. Design, develop, and implement technology-rich professional learning programs that model principles of adult learning and promote digital age best practices in teaching, learning, and assessment.

ISTE STANDARDS•C, 4c. Evaluate results of professional learning programs to determine their effectiveness on deepening teacher content knowledge, improving teacher pedagogical skills, and/or increasing student learning.

Through his work at School Works Enterprises, Olusola Dawodu has played a key role in designing, delivering, and evaluating technology-related professional learning for many teachers in the state of Lagos in southeastern Nigeria.

School Works is a private professional development and consulting company working exclusively with schools. Over the past three years, School Works has been involved in a large-scale project funded by the World Bank and the Lagos Ministry of Education named the Lagos Eko Project (in the Yoruba language, the word 'Eko' means learning). Through the Eko Project, School Works has helped more than 1,500 teachers from over 300 schools in Lagos integrate instructional software and web-based instructional resources into their classroom practices.

The Ministry of Education conducts needs assessments and establishes goals for the Eko Project, while Dawodu's role is to develop and deliver training options based on ISTE's Standards•T for Eko teachers. He also conducts follow-up visits to participating schools from two to three months after teachers have received training. On these visits, Dawodu observes classroom practices, determines if teachers have been able to apply what they have learned, provides individual coaching to teachers who need additional assistance, and uses the information from site visits to inform future professional development strategies.

Dawodu believes the project and others like it are very important to the economic future of students around the world: "Education must prepare students to live and work in the 21st century. We must prepare our students for jobs that may not have been created yet. Graduates must be productive, think critically, and know how to solve problems—as described in the ISTE Standards•S. Employers want to hire people who are already responsible digital citizens. To achieve the ISTE Standards•S, we must first address the ISTE Standards•T. This is why what School Works does is critical."

TABLE 4.1. Technology Coaching Rubric for Standard 4

Standard 4. Professional Development and Program Evaluation.
Technology coaches conduct needs assessments, develop technology-related professional learning programs, and evaluate their impacts on instructional practice and student learning.ng of all students.

a. **Needs Assessment.** Conduct needs assessments to inform the content and delivery of technology-related professional learning programs that result in a positive impact on student learning.

b. **Professional Learning.** Design, develop, and implement technology-rich professional learning programs that model principles of adult learning and promote digital age best practices in teaching, learning, and assessment.

c. **Program Evaluation.** Evaluate results of professional learning programs to determine their effectiveness on deepening teacher content knowledge, improving teacher pedagogical skills, and/or increasing student learning.

Approaches	Meets	Exceeds
TECHNOLOGY COACHES: • identify research-based principles of adult learning and standards for high-quality professional development/evaluation. (4a–c) • identify best-practice examples of how these principles and standards have been implemented to support the effective use of technology in K–12 schools. (4a–c)	TECHNOLOGY COACHES: • conduct needs assessments to inform the content and delivery of technology-related professional learning programs that result in a positive impact on student learning. (4a) • design, develop, and implement technology-rich professional learning programs that model principles of adult learning and promote digital age best practices in teaching, learning, and assessment. (4b) • evaluate results of professional learning programs to determine the effectiveness on deepening teacher content knowledge, improving teacher pedagogical skills, and/or increasing student learning. (4c)	TECHNOLOGY COACHES: • provide evidence that technology-related professional development programs increased or improved the use of technology in the classroom and/or improved student learning. (4a–c) • produce resources related to technology-related professional development and program evaluation that are used by educators beyond their local school. (4a–c)

Performances in Professional Development and Program Evaluation

The ISTE Technology Coaching Rubric describes performances that approach, meet, and exceed expectations for ISTE Standards•C, Standard Four: Professional Development and Program Evaluation. This section is designed to provide an explanation of the rubric as related to Standard Four and to provide more examples in each category.

Table 4.1 illustrates how coaches can have positive effects on professional development and program evaluation. Note the differences in performances among the approaches, meets, and exceeds levels.

APPROACHES

Peter has accepted a position as a technology coach after serving as a high school English teacher for 10 years. To prepare for his new job, he is reading about professional development for teachers and adult learning. He is especially interested in studying the most effective techniques for helping his colleagues learn and comparing them to those for teaching teenagers.

Samantha is a technology specialist in her school district, which is proposing to implement a 1:1 initiative at her school next year. To prepare for that initiative, Samantha has been gathering information about how different districts have successfully helped teachers prepare for the influx of technology.

Bonnie, who has been a technology coach for two years, wants to improve her ability to document and communicate the successes of her professional development efforts. She also wants to become more skillful in gathering ongoing information that will improve her practice. To work toward achieving these goals, Bonnie has enrolled in a program evaluation course through her local university.

MEETS

Caroline is a full-time technology coach who has just transferred to a new school. To begin her work, she visits each grade-level team and asks them a series of questions. The questions are designed to help Caroline determine how much technology is being used, how she might help teachers reach district goals, and what teachers are most interested in learning. She plans to use this information to develop a customized professional learning plan for the school.

Darien is a university professor who has partnered with a local school to enhance students' knowledge and skills related to science, technology, engineering, and math. To pursue those goals, Darien has received a $250,000 grant to fund professional development for STEM teachers. In cooperation with the school's tech coach, Darien is designing a professional development program that includes online training, teacher stipends for curriculum development, in-class coaching for teachers, and teachers' reflections at the end of the year.

Tomás is a part-time technology coach who helps teachers use a new student information system. To evaluate the effectiveness of his work, he sets specific goals for teachers› usage and monitors progress toward the goals. By collecting ongoing information, he is able to identify and help teachers who are not up to speed or are confused about the new system.

Yoli is a full-time technology coach who supports a digital age pilot school. Students attending this school have access to tech tools and experience digital teaching methods that their counterparts in the district›s other schools do not yet have. To evaluate the impact of the program on student achievement, Yoli will compare standardized test scores from the pilot group to similar groups of students in other schools. She will also compare students' individual achievement gains during the first pilot year to their progress in previous years.

EXCEEDS

McKenzie is a full-time technology coach who documented case studies of how she had helped teachers move to higher-levels of technology integration. She shared these success stories in her annual review with her supervisor and received an exemplary performance rating.

Zane is a language arts teacher who provided training and coaching to his grade-level team on how to use graphic organizer software to help struggling writers. Teachers used the program, and the majority of the students' writing samples showed great growth from the beginning to the end of the year. Zane worked closely with two of his colleagues, coaching them in finding ways to help a few students who weren't responding well the program. Eventually, those students caught on to using the software and experienced success. Several students dramatically improved their scores on state-mandated writing exams.

Ron is an experienced, full-time technology coach. Knowing that evaluating professional learning is challenging, Ron compiled a list of practical ways to document teachers' new knowledge and skills, changes in classroom practice, and improved student learning. He published his ideas on his blog and presented them at several conferences. Other technology coaches appreciated Ron's work and implemented his ideas with great success.

Whitney is a full-time technology coach for a state department of education. After several years of designing, developing, and implementing online programs for teachers' professional development, she created a series of video tips for supporting teachers in virtual environments. She posted the videos online, and the videos were viewed around the world. Several universities asked Whitney for permission to include her videos in their courses' content. Other state departments of education have asked her to help them start teacher online learning communities.

Discussion Questions for Professional Development and Program Evaluation

1. What was your favorite professional learning experience?

2. What qualities made the experience great?

3. How would you assess the quality of technology-related professional learning in your organization? What could be improved and how?

4. What do you think about the gamification of professional learning? If you have experienced interactive games as part of your development program, explain how they enhanced (or did not enhance) your learning. Would you like to try participating in group simulations as part of your professional learning? How could you build your skills to implement gamified professional learning?

5. What are your experiences with online professional learning? What are the pros and cons? What would you need to learn to implement online professional learning opportunities?

6. How would you describe the differences between formal and informal professional learning? How could you help create a culture of continual learning and sharing among teachers?

7. Do you agree that coaching is a powerful component of professional learning? Why or why not? Which coaching strategies do you use? Describe strategies you would add to the list presented in this chapter.

Essential Conditions Connection—ISTE Essential Conditions and ISTE Standards•C, Standard 4

When enacting Standard Four—Professional Development and Program Evaluation—technology coaches support the following essential conditions:

- **Skilled Personnel**
- **Ongoing Professional Learning**
- **Assessment and Evaluation**

TABLE 4.2. ISTE Essential Conditions Related to ISTE Standards•C, 4

ISTE Essential Conditions	ISTE STANDARDS•C 4. Teaching, Learning, and Assessment
SKILLED PERSONNEL Educators, support staff, and other leaders are skilled in the selection and effective use of appropriate ICT resources. ONGOING PROFESSIONAL LEARNING Educators have ongoing access to technology-related professional learning plans and opportunities as well as dedicated time to practice and share ideas.	Needs Assessment (ISTE Standards•C, 4a) Professional Learning (ISTE Standards•C, 4b) When technology coaches conduct needs assessments and design/deliver professional learning opportunities for educators, they are providing ongoing professional learning and contribute to a skilled workforce able to implement digital age learning.
ASSESSMENT AND EVALUATION Teaching, learning, leadership, and the use of ICT and digital resources are continually assessed and evaluated.	Program Evaluation (ISTE Standards•C, 4c) Technology coaches evaluate the impact of professional development efforts on deepening teacher content knowledge, improving teacher pedagogical skills, changing classroom practice, and/or increasing student learning.

8. Do you feel prepared to evaluate the impact of professional learning on teachers' learning, classroom practice changes, and student achievement? Why or why not? What additional support do you need to become more confident as an evaluator?

Resources for Professional Development and Program Evaluation

ISTE Coaching White Paper

ISTE has published a 21-page white paper titled Technology, Coaching and Community: Power Partners for Improved Professional Development in Primary and Secondary Education. This publication is free to ISTE members and available to nonmembers as an ISTE resource. **www.iste.org/resources/product?ID=2157**

Learning Forward

Learning Forward is a professional organization serving a broad variety of educators who specialize in helping in-service teachers learn. The organization was formerly known as the National Staff Development Council (NSDC). Learning Forward is well regarded for publishing standards for high-quality professional learning.

> http://learningforward.org
>
> http://learningforward.org/standards-for-professional-learning

Students as Coaches

Generation YES is a program that trains students to provide technical and curricular support functions in schools. Generation Yes empowers students to shape technology programs in schools and support educators in digital age learning environments. The organization also supports project-based learning, tech integration, and data collection and assessment.

> http://genyes.org

BOOKS ON INSTRUCTIONAL COACHING

A selection of books related to coaching in K–12 schools is listed below. While the books are not specifically geared to technology, they are applicable to the work that technology coaches do. Knight's book is a favorite for coaches who want to understand and improve their practices. Killion and her coauthors' book provides a good justification of why coaching is necessary, how to support coaching practices in schools, and is a useful resource for those who supervise coaches or want to see coaching practices emerge in their organizations.

> Aguilar, E. (2003). *The art of coaching: Effective strategies for school transformation.* San Francisco, CA: Jossey-Bass.
>
> Killion, J., Harrison, C., Bryan, C., & Clifton, H. (2012). *Coaching matters.* Oxford, OH: Learning Forward.
>
> Knight, J. (2007). *Instructional coaching.* Thousand Oaks, CA: Corwin.
>
> Marzano, R. J., & Simms, J. A. (2013). *Coaching classroom instruction.* Bloomington, IN: Marzano Research Laboratory.

BOOKS ON PROFESSIONAL LEARNING

Though coaching is a highly effective model for professional learning, technology coaches need to implement other types of professional learning activities. The following books explore a variety of options for teachers' professional development.

> Borthwick, A., & Pearson, M. (2008). *Transforming classroom practice: Professional development strategies in educational technology.* Eugene, OR: ISTE.
>
> Easton, L. B. (2008). *Powerful designs for professional learning* (2nd ed.). Oxford, OH: National Staff Development Council.
>
> Phelps, R., & Graham, A. (2013). *Technology together: Whole-school professional development for capability and confidence.* Eugene, OR: ISTE.

BOOK ON PROGRAM EVALUATION

Killion's book is an essential handbook for technology coaches. Its step-by-step instructions describe how to design high-quality evaluations of professional learning programs.

> Killion, J. (2008). *Assessing impact: Evaluating staff development* (2nd ed.). Thousand Oaks, CA: Corwin.

PROFESSIONAL LEARNING NETWORKS

Not all professional learning is achieved through coaching, workshops, or training. High-quality professional learning also occurs through informal, self-directed collaboration with a group of peers and mentors. This group is often referred to as a personal or professional learning network (PLN) or professional learning community (PLC). Of course, technology offers the opportunity to expand PLNs. The following book provides a step-by-step guide for developing online PLNs. Technology coaches can use this book to help others develop PLNs or to enrich their own face-to-face and blended connections.

> Thompson, R. C., Kitchie, L. C., & Gagnon, R. J. (2011). *Constructing an online professional learning network for school unity and student achievement.* Thousand Oaks, CA: Corwin.

CHAPTER 5

Digital Citizenship

ISTE STANDARDS•C, STANDARD 5
Digital Citizenship

Technology coaches model and promote digital citizenship.

Though we may think we understand what it means to be a good citizen, have our definitions changed? Has our increasing reliance on technology perhaps changed our thought processes and behaviors? Most of us would agree that good citizens not only heed laws, but also follow policies and norms of behavior that benefit the common good and preserve an orderly society. By doing so, good citizens protect themselves and others from harm. In turn, they expect others to behave in the same ways.

What it means to be a responsible citizen appears to have changed over the past few decades, as new situations and circumstances have presented themselves. The advent of information and communication technologies has triggered the need to redefine good citizenship in many ways. In fact, the term *digital citizenship* has been coined to describe responsible actions for technology leaders and users.

Technology holds great promise for expanding and enhancing students' educational opportunities. Technology also holds great dangers if used inappropriately. In an era of rapid change, technology coaches must help educators, students, parents, and other stakeholders understand how to maximize the benefits and minimize the perils of technology use. Technology coaches accomplish this by (1) modeling good citizenship in everything they do, (2) directly teaching digital citizenship concepts, and (3) advocating for the advancement of digital citizenship in their schools.

Since it is difficult to predict how educators and students will use new technologies, technology coaches should also be prepared to understand emerging issues and shape technology use for the common good. Technology coaches will continue to contribute to the formation of new policies and guidelines that will structure school technology programs in positive ways.

ISTE Standards • C, Standard Five contains three elements that, taken together, define digital citizenship. Technology coaches must understand and be able to model and promote these elements:

- Digital Equity

- Safe, Healthy, Legal, and Ethical Uses

- Diversity, Cultural Understanding, and Global Awareness

Digital Equity

ISTE STANDARDS•C, 5a
Digital Equity

Model and promote strategies for achieving equitable access to digital tools and resources and technology-related best practices for all students and teachers.

The quest for digital equity is a long-standing issue in educational technology. At the most basic level, digital equity in education is typically framed in terms of providing teachers and students with equitable access to computers and high-speed internet access at school. Of course, definitions of "adequate school access" are relative and shifting. Some educators are still striving to meet basic levels of school connectivity. In contrast, other educators are launching 1:1 initiatives, where all students have connected, personal computing devices to support their own learning. Digital equity in education usually means closing a *digital divide* between students who have access to computers and high-speed internet access at school and those who do not. Around the world, educators in many developing countries and isolated areas are still striving to achieve basic access levels. In developed countries, educators agree that they need more computers and wider bandwidth to achieve advanced levels of technology-supported instruction. Many educators believe schools will not fully maximize technology for learning until all students have a connected, personal computing device to support their own learning at school and at home.

While school access to computers and the internet is a critical first step, conversations around providing true digital equity for students have expanded to other dimensions. These dimensions include, but are not necessarily limited, to the following:

- **Access to other types of technology at school.** Free internet content and web-based productivity tools are extremely useful, but they may not have the qualities, functionalities, and/or security features needed for educational settings. For these reasons, students and teachers also need access to technologies such as printers, digital microscopes and probes, productivity tools, content-based software, assistive technologies, assessment tools, online subscription-based resources, and online learning courses. Since securing these digital learning resources requires funding and expertise, it may be difficult for many schools to acquire them. Technology coaches can help bridge this gap.

They can examine the technologies other schools have, explore what is available to support their schools' curriculums, and advocate for the purchase of beneficial products in their schools.

- **Opportunities to use technology at school.** Researchers have suggested that students from both lower and higher socioeconomic schools (SES) use technology frequently, but the patterns of use may be different. For example, researchers have found that students at lower SES schools are more likely to use computers for remediation, reinforcement of skills, and independent work, while their counterparts at wealthier schools reported using a wider range of technologies in more advanced ways, including producing and sharing original products. Special education students have been cited as another subgroup that may lag behind other students in digital learning opportunities. To promote equity, coaches should examine the context of use in their local schools and advocate for student technology use as represented in the ISTE Standards for Students (ISTE Standards • S). Students who use technology for communicating, gathering information, collaborating, solving problems, analyzing information, and presenting to real audiences are more likely to develop technology skills with economic and civic values.

- **Beyond school access to computers and high-speed internet.** Students without modern computing devices and high-speed internet beyond the school day have less ability to engage in anywhere, anytime learning than their counterparts with greater access. In international studies of digital equity, wealth and education levels are repeatedly associated with higher levels of computer ownership and connectivity. The availability and cost of high-speed internet in specific geographical regions also influence beyond-school access. For example, in the United States, access levels in rural areas and in some states tend to lag behind national averages. Technology coaches should help their colleagues understand and improve students' beyond school access.

- **Access to knowledge networks.** In addition to access to technologies, students need access to knowledgeable mentors and peers who will help them develop technology literacy. Research suggests that students from higher socioeconomic schools have greater access to these types of social support and to wider varieties of high-quality print and online technical support resources as well. As a result, students from wealthier schools and families are more likely to develop advanced understandings of technology and to have greater confidence in their technical abilities. Technology coaches can promote the development of knowledge networks through strategies such as student technology clubs, community mentors, and teachers' professional development.

- **Access to culturally and linguistically relevant digital content.** Access to computers, the internet, and digital learning resources lack impact unless culturally and linguistically relevant content is available to learners. In general, content such as websites, instructional videos, and educational software target dominant cultures and speakers of English. Highly technical materials are often thought to be more attractive to males. As a result of these oversights or stereotypes, students from minority groups and female students may lack digital content relating to their native languages or cultural experiences. Technology coaches can respond to these inequities by asking publishers to consider diversity when developing and marketing products. They can also encourage culturally and linguistically diverse students and their teachers to create and publish digital content that has personal meanings for themselves and others.

- **Access to content for learners with disabilities.** High-quality learning materials are useful only when all learners can access them. Inequities exist when learners with disabilities cannot receive the same benefits from technology-supported learning as their counterparts. To minimize inequities, technology equipment and technology-based learning materials must be universally accessible. For example, tech coaches can ask teachers to use videos with optional captioning and print materials available in formats accessible for screen readers.

These dimensions help illustrate the complexity of digital equity. Assessing and addressing ISTE Standards • C, 5a is a challenging, evolving task. Technology coaches must monitor all aspects of digital equity in their schools, advocate for all students, and model strategies for equalizing the playing field.

TECHNOLOGY COACHING CASE STUDY

From Promoting Basic Access to Modeling Cultural and Global Awareness of Digital Tools

—Anwar Abdulbaki
Online Education Coordinator
REACH OUT TO ASIA
DOHA, QATAR

ISTE STANDARDS•C, 5a: Model and promote strategies for achieving equitable access to digital tools and resources and technology-related best practices for all students and teachers.

ISTE STANDARDS•C, 5c: Model and promote diversity, cultural understanding, and global awareness by using digital age communication and collaboration tools to interact locally and globally with students, peers, parents, and the larger community.

Anwar Abdulbaki is the online education coordinator for Reach Out to Asia (ROTA), a not-for-profit organization in Qatar committed to improving education in crisis-affected areas.

ROTA project schools exhibit extreme needs. Abdulbaki has worked with earthquake victims, educators whose schools have been destroyed by bombs, and refugees who have been displaced from their homes. In such cases, ROTA begins its work by establishing basic access to educational resources.

When ROTA identifies a crisis-affected area, Abdulbaki usually participates in on-site assessment visits and provides input on what information and communication technologies (ICTs) and training programs are necessary for schools. Upon returning to his office, he writes proposals to buy or refurbish equipment to be shipped to project schools, and he recommends professional development strategies.

Abdulbaki also spends many hours developing a network of educators interested in online learning, identifying online learning opportunities for educators, and training them to participate in these projects. In this aspect of his job, he works with both high-need and highly developed schools. "Schools in the Qatar iEarn network, for example, are very advanced and well-equipped, but it is important to develop these stable online collaborators for the schools in crisis when they are ready to participate," he explains.

He works with a network of educators in more than 130 countries. He co-coordinates the Qatar iEarn network, and he helped coordinate the 'Beirut39' Project, a project honoring 39 Arab writers under 39 years of age.

Abdulbaki believes that the most powerful applications of ICT help improve all learners' access to quality education and enable them to collaborate with others beyond the walls of classrooms: "This makes learning more meaningful and relevant to students. Students can communicate with those from other cultures and develop cross-cultural understanding, which is very critical for life and work in the 21st century."

Safe, Healthy, Legal, and Ethical Uses

ISTE STANDARDS•C, 5b
Safe, Healthy, Legal, and Ethical Uses

Model and facilitate safe, healthy, legal, and ethical uses of digital information and technologies.

As a top priority in meeting this standard, technology coaches are entrusted to ensure that they promote lawful technology use as prescribed for them in their local settings. U.S. educational technology programs are also bound by the following pieces of federal legislation and all subsequent amendments to these laws:

- The Family Educational Rights and Privacy Act (FERPA, 1974)

- The Copyright Act of 1976 (amended in 1998 and in 2002)

- The Rehabilitation Act of 1978 (amended in 1998)

- The Americans with Disabilities Act (ADA, 1990, amended in 2008)

- The Children's Online Privacy and Protection Act (COPPA, 2000)

- The Children's Internet Protection Act (CIPA, 2001)

- The Individuals with Disabilities in Education Act (IDEA, 2004)

These federal laws address keeping students safe online, meeting the technology needs of students with disabilities, and protecting intellectual property. In addition to these laws, many states have passed laws related to online learning requirements, cyberbullying, hacking, and other issues related to appropriate technology use in educational settings. Table 5.1 outlines some of the laws related to technology in education.

While ensuring compliance with federal and state laws is an important first step for tech coaches, they need to understand that legislation often addresses issues in broad terms. Though many other matters related to the healthy, safe, and ethical uses of technology are not legislated, they are very important. For example, responsible users demonstrate proper etiquette during online communication, maintain an appropriate digital identity, keep school district technology equipment in good working order, and balance their screen time with other important activities. School districts and numerous organizations have become increasingly interested in promoting ergonomically healthy uses of technology to prevent injuries and in employing environmentally friendly technology practices to protect and conserve resources.

A second step for tech coaches in U.S. school districts is to write or update a clear list of technology behaviors (dos and don'ts) expected of technology users, including consequences that will be enforced if the rules are broken. These lists of good behaviors and consequences for unacceptable conduct related to tech use are called acceptable use policies (AUPs) or responsible use policies (RUPs). To formalize these agreements, school employees, students, and parents are asked to agree in writing to terms of the district's AUPs or RUPs annually.

Technology coaches help others understand and apply the relevant laws and principles—including but not limited to the district's AUP or RUP—related to the safe, healthy, legal, and ethical uses of technology. Because of their proximity to best practices, technology coaches raise awareness by talking about these issues and modeling best practices. Technology coaches also make valuable contributions to drafting AUPs/RUPs and helping to educate others.

TABLE 5.1. U.S. Laws' Influences on Technology Use in Schools

Examples of U.S. Laws Influencing Technology Use in Schools
Children's Internet Protection Act (CIPA, 2001) The Children's Internet Protection Act (CIPA) requires schools to enact technology protection measures, monitor students' internet activity, and educate minors on internet safety. CIPA requires schools to have an Internet Safety Policy (ISP) addressing the following: • Access by minors to inappropriate matter on the internet; • The safety and security of minors when using electronic mail, chat rooms, and other forms of direct electronic communications; • Unauthorized access, including so-called hacking, and other unlawful activities by minors online; • Unauthorized disclosure, use, and dissemination of personal information regarding minors; and • Measures restricting minors' access to materials harmful to them • To comply with CIPA, most school districts use filtering software to block harmful content and rely on educators to provide additional monitoring and education on internet safety. Since CIPA requires at least one public hearing on internet safety policies, districts usually place their ISP on a Board of Education agenda and seek formal approval for the document. School districts are not eligible to receive technology-related federal funding, such as e-Rate, unless they can show evidence of CIPA compliance.
The Individuals with Disabilities in Education Act (IDEA, 2004) The IDEA is a comprehensive set of rules and regulations that extend far beyond technology-related issues. While technology coaches do not need to become IDEA experts, they do need to understand its components related to assistive technologies. This knowledge will help technology coaches collaborate with special education leaders in their district. According to this law, schools must provide necessary assistive technologies and assistive technology services to students with disabilities as needed at home and at school. At times, schools must also provide assistive technologies and services to students' teachers and parents—all free of charge to students and their families. IDEA defines assistive technologies and dictates when providing technologies and services are deemed necessary. Schools are provided funding to implement IDEA. Federal guidance for IDEA is issued through and funding is authorized by the U.S. Department of Education (US-ED). Updates and official information for IDEA can be obtained through its website. To receive funds, state departments of education or state education agencies develop plans for IDEA funds and apply for their allocations. Local school districts receive their funds from state agencies. These IDEA funds are usually managed by district-level special education departments.

Sections 504 and 508 of the Rehabilitation Act of 1978 (amended in 1998)

The Rehabilitation Act is a broad civil rights law that protects all disabled Americans from discrimination.

Section 504 specifically addresses the responsibility of federally funded schools to provide disabled children with a free and appropriate public education. Unlike IDEA, no funding is provided specifically for schools through the Rehabilitation Act. The definition of what qualifies as a disability is broader than the definition in IDEA. Because of this, students can sometimes qualify for services, including assistive technology, under the Rehabilitation Act even if they do not qualify under IDEA. Because it is a broader law, the Rehabilitation Act is administered the U.S. Department of Health and Human Services, Office of Civil Rights. However, the U.S. Department of Education requires any school receiving federal education funds (including IDEA and many other programs) to certify compliance with Section 504.

Section 508 of the Rehabilitation Act mandates that government agencies must provide disabled individuals with equal access to public information, including web-based resources, unless doing so creates an undue burden.

To date, K–12 schools have not been considered government agencies, and the US-ED has not required schools to certify Section 508 compliance. However, exponential growth of online learning has refocused interest in universal access and design. Court cases have challenged universities to make content more accessible, and legislators have proposed laws expanding accessibility requirements in higher education. Many predict that similar actions in K–12 education will follow.

For these reasons, school technology leaders should consider accessibility of all technology-based websites and products developed, used, or purchased in the school system. Certainly, schools want their students, parents, teachers, and community members to have equitable access to all teaching, learning, and information resources and should be working toward that goal.

Americans with Disabilities Act (ADA, 1990, amended in 2008)

The ADA is a broad attempt to eliminate discrimination against individuals with disabilities—especially in the workplace. This law is administered by the Civil Rights Office of the United States Department of Justice. It extends to the private sector, not only to the public sector receiving federal funds. ADA does not really add anything to IDEA or the Rehabilitation Act pertaining to school-age children, and it does not provide funding to schools. It simply reinforces the legal mandates in IDEA and Section 504 of the Rehabilitation Act and extends them to other populations. Although less relevant for educators, the ADA shares some common definitions of assistive technology with IDEA and the Rehabilitation Act. It is good for technology coaches to know those definitions and understand how ADA fits into the federal legislation landscape related to disabilities. In some situations, ADA might apply to school employees, parents, or other constituents.

Family Educational Rights and Privacy Act (FERPA, 1974)

The Family Educational Rights and Privacy Act (FERPA) centers on students' information records. While the legislation is not focused on technology-related issues, digital age storage and sharing of information adds new dimensions to protecting students' privacy. FERPA provides guidelines on who can access student information and what types of information can be published.

For example, FERPA allows schools to give particular school employees and external contractors with *legitimate educational interest* access to students' data without [those students' or their parents'] consent, but the employees or contractors must keep the data confidential. Under these guidelines, external software contractors would be allowed to store student information on behalf of the school, but only to use that information within the scope of that contract.

FERPA also allows schools to share directory information, including a student's name, address, telephone number, date and place of birth, honors and awards, and dates of attendance. However, schools must inform parents and students how the directory information will be shared and allow them to opt out if they want more privacy. This means schools must inform parents as to what information will be published on the school's website and allow them the opportunity to decline. Schools usually lean on existing publication policies for newspapers, yearbooks, and promotional videos to inform their web-publishing policies.

FERPA requires schools to notify parents and students of their rights under FERPA on an annual basis. For ease of administration, schools usually add this information to student/parent handbooks distributed at the start of school each year.

See the U.S. Department of Education's website (www2.ed.gov/policy/gen/guid/fpco/ferpa/index.html) for guidance on FERPA.

Children's Online Privacy and Protection Act (COPPA, 2000)

COPPA is primarily directed toward commercial websites. It restricts the online collection of personal information from minors under age 13 without the express consent of a parent or guardian. Because of COPPA, detailed 'terms of use' for minors can usually be found on reputable websites; users are asked to provide names, phone numbers, mailing addresses, and/or email addresses. To comply with COPPA, some websites ask users to certify that they are over 13 years old before registering for the site. Others allow minors to create an account but require parental permission first. Technology coaches should be able to find these terms of use and help their colleagues figure out how to comply with them. In many cases, the online providers will offer upgraded service options that protect the anonymity and/or privacy of young users. In other cases, educators must seek parental permission for students to use particular products or find alternatives. Prezi, Edmodo, and Facebook are good case studies for exploring terms of use. Neither COPPA nor CIPA should be confused with the Children's Online Protection Act (COPA, 1998), an earlier federal law that has never taken effect and was declared unconstitutional by the courts because it prohibits much more speech than is necessary.

Copyright Act of 1976 (amended many times, including in 1998, 2002)

Understanding copyright legislation in the United States begins with the Copyright Act of 1976. However, this law has been amended many times, including the Digital Millennium Copyright Act in 1998, and the Technology, Education, and Copyright Harmonization Act of 2002. While the content of copyright law is complex and extensive, the intentions of the law are rather simple. Copyright legislation protects authors' original works so that innovation and creativity will continue to flourish. Of particular interest to educators is the concept of fair use. Technology coaches must help educators and students understand the principles of copyright and why it is important to respect this law. By promoting good copyright practices, technology coaches teach others to (1) find copyright-compliant material for multimedia projects, (2) properly cite original sources, (3) seek permission from authors to use their work, and (4) protect the rights to their own original materials. Technology coaches also help ensure that proper licenses, documentation, and password usage are in place for installed software and purchased, web-based subscriptions in their schools.

TECHNOLOGY COACHING CASE STUDY

Revolutionizing Responsible Use and Internet Safety

—Christine Haynes
ICT Coordinator
IMMANUEL PRIMARY SCHOOL
NOVAR GARDENS, SOUTH AUSTRALIA

ISTE STANDARDS•C, 5a: Model and promote strategies for achieving equitable access to digital tools and resources and technology-related best practices for all students and teachers.

ISTE STANDARDS•C, 5b: Model and facilitate safe, healthy, legal, and ethical uses of digital information and technologies.

Christine Haynes was awarded the Australian Council for Computers in Education "Educator of the Year" in 2013. On a day-to-day basis, she is responsible for coordinating the ICT program for more than 600 students in prekindergarten through year six. Her work involves a little bit of everything—professional development for teachers, IT management, and directly teaching students.

Since the Australian government launched the Digital Education Revolution in 2008, Haynes' job has expanded. The goals of this initiative include lowering student-to-computer ratios and expanding connectivity in Australian classrooms. As student access to technology increases, Haynes reports a growing need to help students be responsible, productive digital citizens.

One of her first actions was to put students' names on their personal laptops and to help them develop a shared responsibility for these resources: "Students need ownership of the devices. They need to see technology as a critical e-learning tool and take the responsibility to care for it. After all, no one washes a rental car!"

Haynes also began teaching the government-supported Cybersmart curriculum to students. She coordinated two units per grade level with the teachers and administrators and enhanced the curriculum with guest speakers, discussions, scenarios, and role play.

She also has helped student representatives from her school participate in the Australian Youth Advisory Group (YAG) on Cyber Safety. Students in the YAG provide input on cybersafety issues to the Australian Department of Education.

The YAG has already had a direct impact on policy and products. For example, the government has developed a CyberSafety help button that can be downloaded and installed on any website. When selected, the button launches an internet safety user guide.

Haynes hopes her efforts to promote responsible use and internet safety will help students at her school maximize the benefits of technology for learning and avoid potential dangers.

TECHNOLOGY COACHING CASE STUDY

Copyright Coach Focuses on What Students CAN Do

—Mrs. Geri Kimoto
Middle School Librarian
KAMEHAMEHA SCHOOLS MAUI
PUKALANI, HAWAII

ISTE STANDARDS•C, 5b: Model and facilitate safe, healthy, legal, and ethical uses of digital information and technologies.

To help teachers and students at her school use safe, healthy, legal, and ethical technology practices, middle school librarian Geri Kimoto prefers to coach students and teachers when they need support.

For example, when the students and teachers have projects requiring them to integrate multimedia resources, they frequently come to Kimoto for assistance: "What they really want is to find the photos or music they need, but I also see this as an opportunity to help them understand copyright."

Kimoto knows there are federal laws and school policies on safe, legal, and ethical uses of technology, but she believes that the guidelines don't make much sense to teachers and students unless they have opportunities to apply them.

She also observes that teachers and students sometimes see these regulations as restricting and annoying but tries to reshape their thinking. "What teachers and students need are examples of what they can do, what they can use, and how to appropriately give credit to authors," she explained.

To help teachers and students gain this understanding, Kimoto shows them resources, such as Creative Commons, to illustrate the different ways authors and publishers are willing to share their work. On her blog, she also posts links to music and image websites that are copyright-friendly for educational purposes.

Through her efforts, Kimoto believes teachers and students learn to respect the intellectual property of others, while creating excellent, original products. As a next step, she hopes to help students share their own work with broader audiences. She believes this will help students understand copyright from the perspective of a knowledge creator: "This will really help them see how authors feel!"

Common Issues Related to the Safe, Healthy, Legal, and Ethical Uses of Technology

Technology coaches encounter a host of issues when they try to model and facilitate safe, healthy, legal, and ethical uses of technology in schools. These issues include, but are not necessarily limited to the following:

- Promoting ergonomic uses of technology to prevent injury

- Supporting the technology needs of students with disabilities

- Helping students balance screen time with other important activities

- Helping students stay safe online

- Helping students develop proper etiquette for online communications

- Protecting school technology investments from theft and damage

- Protecting privacy of student information

- Avoiding copyright infringement

- Preventing harmful technology uses such as hacking, sexting, and cyberbullying

- Using and disposing of technologies in ways that protect the environment

Teaching Students about Copyright

Creative Commons is a not-for-profit organization that allows users (1) to select a copyright license for their original work and (2) to search for royalty-free pictures, music, videos, and other media. It is also a great teaching tool in the classroom! Here are two ideas for using Creative Commons:

1. Students can practice choosing copyright licenses for their original work. This process will teach them to make decisions, such as: (a) whether or not they will allow others to use their work; (b) under what conditions others can use their work (commercial

or noncommercial, with or without attribution); and (c) whether or not others will be allowed to use and modify their work. Through this activity, students learn to identify with authors and artists rather than consumers. This activity might be best used as a simulation. While minors can actually choose to register a copyright for their work, it is wise—and often mandated by school district policy—to involve parents in decisions about posting original material on the internet, whether or not to use students' real names, and what kind of copyright to choose. Creative Commons' copyright licenses are not revocable (see https://creativecommons.org/licenses).

2. Creative Commons links to many media sharing sites that use its licenses. This allows students to search for appropriate, high-quality music, sounds, pictures, and videos for their multimedia projects. Creative Commons' licenses help students know whether or not they can share the resource for noncommercial uses, whether or not they need to cite the work, and if they may share it whether they can modify it. Searches can also be done through individual sites, such as Jamendo, Flickr, and Google Images.

3. Of course, not every picture, sound, or song has a Creative Commons license, and not all authors or artists grant open permission to use their work. In these situations, students will have to seek permission. On his Landmarks for Schools website, David Warlick has posted a sample template for students who want to pursue permission to use someone else's work (www.landmark-project.com/permission_student.php).

Diversity, Cultural Understanding, and Global Awareness

ISTE STANDARDS•C, 5c

Diversity, Cultural Understanding, and Global Awareness

Model and promote diversity, cultural understanding, and global awareness by using digital age communication and collaboration tools to interact locally and globally with students, peers, parents, and the larger community.

Teachers are expected to help their students understand the benefits of diversity and learn to work with people different from themselves. Teachers are also expected to meet the needs of culturally and linguistically diverse learners in their classrooms. Culturally responsive pedagogy includes establishing student-centered learning environments, where the strengths and interests of learners provide the foundations for instruction. Another hallmark of culturally responsive pedagogy is tapping into family and community funds of knowledge to support the educational process.

Digital age communication and collaboration tools allow students to engage with others from different cultures and to encounter viewpoints, beliefs, and ideas different from their own. With technology and knowledgeable adults to guide them, students from different cultures can collaborate on work, have meaningful discussions, and build mutual understanding that will prepare them for the future.

Technology can also help culturally and linguistically diverse students to find resources matched with their interests, connect with family and community resources outside the school, and publish original work representing their unique opinions and perspectives.

Technology coaches locate these technologies and model how they can be used to support diversity, cultural understanding, and global awareness. Coaches also help teachers implement these technologies and techniques.

TECHNOLOGY COACHING CASE STUDY

Modeling the Teaching of Cultural Understanding via Communication and Collaboration Tools

—Daniel de León

Modern Language Instructor and Educational Technology Coordinator
SANDIA PREPARATORY SCHOOL
ALBUQUERQUE, NEW MEXICO

ISTE STANDARDS•C, 5c: Model and promote diversity, cultural understanding, and global awareness by using digital age communication and collaboration tools to interact locally and globally with students, peers, parents, and the larger community.

For the first time, Daniel de León's school is trying to make space for technology coaching. As a start, de León was released from 20% of his Spanish teaching responsibilities to serve as a technology coordinator. Even though he has limited time for coaching, he has developed a strategy to maximize his impact.

Since his goal is to help his school use technology for collaboration, communication, creativity, and global understanding, as outlined in the ISTE Standards•S, he feels he can best do that by modeling these best practices in his classroom and hoping other teachers become interested.

This year, de León is collaborating with another high school Spanish class to plan, promote, and hold an art exhibit celebrating the Mexican holiday of Día de los Muertos (Day of the Dead). Since many students from the collaborating high school are of Mexican ancestry, de León hopes his students will gain a greater understanding of the country's cultural beliefs and practices. The students are using Skype and other communication technologies to share and plan the art exhibit. De León notes that he, too, is learning new vocabulary and regional variations of the holiday from the experience.

Through this example, he hopes other teachers can see the power of community-based, student-centered learning, and he believes that is starting to happen—but in interesting ways: "So far, no other teacher wants to implement the project just as I have done it, but they are interested in components of it. Some want to know how I put students in roles as a production company to produce this exhibit. Some are interested in the collaboration tools, like Skype. I am happy with this! What I wanted was the opportunity to share and promote technology as a way to get beyond the four walls of a classroom and learn. I think that's working."

Next year, de León hopes that his technology coordination role will move to 40% of his responsibilities and that it will keep increasing until he can coach others full time.

TABLE 5.2. Technology Coaching Rubric for Standard 5

Standard 5. Digital Citizenship Technology coaches model and promote digital citizenship.		
a. **Digital Equity.** Model and promote strategies for achieving equitable access to digital tools and resources and technology-related best practices for all students and teachers. b. **Safe, Healthy, Legal, and Ethical Uses.** Model and facilitate safe, healthy, legal, and ethical uses of digital information and technologies. c. **Diversity, Cultural Understanding, and Global Awareness.** Model and promote diversity, cultural understanding, and global awareness by using digital age communication and collaboration tools to interact locally and globally with students, peers, parents, and the larger community.		
Approaches	Meets	Exceeds
TECHNOLOGY COACHES: • identify strategies and best-practice examples for achieving equitable access to digital tools and resources and technology-related best practices for all students and teachers. (5a) • explain key issues, principles, policies, and legislation that define/influence what are considered safe, healthy, legal, and ethical uses of digital information and technologies in K–12 schools. (5b) • identify best-practice examples of how digital age communication and collaboration tools are used to promote diversity, cultural understanding, and global awareness through local and global interactions among students, peers, parents, and the larger community. (5c)	TECHNOLOGY COACHES: • model and promote strategies for achieving equitable access to digital tools and resources and technology-related best practices for all students and teachers. (5a) • model and facilitate safe, healthy, legal, and ethical uses of digital information and technologies. (5b) • model and promote diversity, cultural understanding, and global awareness by using digital age communication and collaboration tools to interact locally and globally with students, peers, parents, and the larger community. (5c)	TECHNOLOGY COACHES: • provide evidence that strategies they implemented have resulted in greater digital equity, respect for diversity, cultural understanding, and global awareness. (5a, 5c) • provide evidence that strategies they have implemented have had an impact on aligning technology-related practices to safe, healthy, legal, and ethical uses of technology. (5b) • produce resources related to digital citizenship that are used by educators beyond their local schools. (5a–c)

Performance in Digital Citizenship

The ISTE Technology Coaching Rubric describes performances that approach, meet, and exceed expectations for ISTE Standards•C, Standard Five: Digital Citizenship. This section is designed to provide an explanation of the rubric as related to Standard Five and to provide more examples in each category.

Table 5.2 illustrates how coaches can have positive effects on digital citizenship. Note the differences in performances among the approaches, meets, and exceeds levels.

APPROACHES

Katherine is an elementary teacher who encouraged her grade-level team to incorporate multimedia projects into the curriculum. While the multimedia projects were highly successful, Katherine noted that students and teachers might have included songs, photos, and large portions of text from copyrighted material. Unsure of the rules herself, she spent several hours learning about copyright guidelines and fair use.

Bernard is a full-time technology coordinator at three middle schools. He is concerned that students do not have equitable access to computers beyond the school day and wonders if there is some way to help the situation. To gather some ideas, he explored what other schools are doing to help bridge the digital divide in students' homes.

Anna is a part-time teacher, part-time technology coach, and an instructional technology graduate student. At a recent conference, she attended a presentation on the dimensions of digital equity and learned that digital equity is not just about access to computers and software at school. Differences in access to beyond-school technologies, social networks to support technology, and opportunities to use technology in advanced ways can also create inequities.

Sarah Beth is a full-time technology coach who wants to support diversity, cultural understanding, and global awareness at her school. As a start, she made a list of collaboration and communication technologies available to students and teachers in her schools. She also found several online resources teachers can use to find classroom partners and collaborators from around the world.

MEETS

Theresa is a middle school media specialist who advocates digital equity in many ways. After talking with some of the families in her school, she learned that they had declined free internet access because they were afraid of the hidden costs and wanted to protect their children's safety at home. To ease their concerns, she held several information sessions. She taught them about the program and gave them different strategies for keeping their children safe online. She also offered a free, six-week computer literacy class for parents who wanted to become more comfortable with computers. The school's community liaison helped Teresa translate the informational materials into several languages and helped co-teach the classes for parents with limited English proficiency.

Helene is a full-time technology coach at a large elementary school. To be compliant with CIPA, her school district asked all third through fifth-grade teachers to incorporate internet safety into the curriculum. To help the teachers, Helene created a webpage with links to instructional resources. She also met with each grade-level team, suggested classroom activities, and co-taught several lessons with the teachers.

Karl noticed that students were using several strategies to bypass the district's filtering software to illegally download music and videos. Teachers were unaware of what students were doing. At a faculty meeting, Karl helped teachers understand why the filtering software was in place, how to monitor students' actions, and what disciplinary actions should occur when students used these sites at school. Because of Karl's help, teachers were able to educate students and reduce unsafe and illegal computer practices in their classrooms.

Hugo is a second grade teacher who addresses learning standards on weather in his class. To help his students understand why different regions have different temperatures and levels of rainfall, he connected with six other classrooms around the world. As students in each classroom reported their weather and rainfall for the day to each other, they noted the differences and investigated why weather differs from region to region. Students also discussed how weather influences the way people dress and what crops they grow. Through this collaboration, students also addressed standards on global understanding. Hugo shared this information with other second grade teachers so they and their students could join the collaboration.

Sandra is a media specialist in a small elementary school. To help the teachers in her school, she made a list of online Web 2.0 tools appropriate for children under 13. These sites did not restrict underage users and did not collect identifiable information. She also asked the district technology director to consider establishing free or low-cost district accounts for several products. By using educational versions, students would be able to participate without submitting personal information, and the environments were more secure. Since some of the products required a contact person, she volunteered to serve as their district administrator.

EXCEEDS

Joanna is an instructional designer in a large university. Her main task is supporting fully online programs. Recently, she helped professors understand the importance of designing learning objects that are accessible to students with disabilities. She educated others on universal design principles, sections 504 and 508 of the Rehabilitation Act, and developments in online learning in other universities across the country. To help professors improve their courses, she consulted with them and connected them to support services for video captioning. As a result of her efforts, online learning materials improved, and the university president presented Joanna with a diversity award.

Barrett is a full-time technology coach. Three years ago, he challenged teachers and students to make their school as paperless as possible. He even helped teachers connect the initiative to key curriculum standards. Driven by student interest, the effort eventually expanded to other environmentally friendly technology practices, such as printer cartridge recycling and reducing energy consumption on computing devices. Students learned math skills by collecting and analyzing data to track their progress. In the most recent school year, paper consumption had declined by 75% since the start of the program, energy costs had declined 15%, and toner costs were nearly cut in half. The superintendent and school board rewarded the school by allocating the cost savings to the school's technology program.

Dallas is a first-year technology coach serving six schools in his district. When he read the district's acceptable use policies (AUPs) for teacher and students, he noticed that the policies hadn't been updated for several years. He also noted that new BYOD initiatives had created new circumstances that were not addressed by the policies. In efforts to improve the policies, Dallas drafted some sample language for future AUPs and met with teachers to discuss his suggestions. After editing his proposal, based on teachers' feedback, he submitted the proposal to the district technology director. Several modifications were made to the AUPs as a result of Dallas' efforts.

Valerie is a regional technology director who wanted to help high school history teachers record and share the experiences of WWII veterans and their families. She wrote a grant proposal that was accepted, and six high schools received funding for professional learning. The professional development program trained teachers and students to conduct interviews and create short video documentaries. Over a period of six years, students gathered stories from diverse audiences and shared their videos online. The project created many meaningful, cross-cultural, and cross-generational connections with local communities. Students and teachers involved in the project won many awards and received recognition for their efforts.

Discussion Questions for Digital Citizenship

1. Do teachers and students have equitable access to modern computing devices, software, and resources at school? Do students use technology in equitable ways?

2. Do students have equitable access to technologies and resources beyond school? How can their home access be determined?

3. If students do not have equitable access, what strategies can be used to close that gap?

4. To what extent do teachers and students in your school understand and comply with copyright law? What can be done to help your community become copyright compliant?

5. To what extent are the web-based content materials created in your school compliant with accessibility guidelines? What can be done to help your community create universally accessible content?

6. To what extent are students practicing safe and ethical computing? What problems exist? How is your school helping students, parents, and teachers to understand the issues and to take responsible, proactive action? What else needs to be done? How can you help?

7. To comply with the Children's Internet Protection Act, most U.S. schools deploy internet filtering software. Sometimes these filters block sites that are educationally beneficial. If a teacher encounters a blocked site, what is the process in your district for allowing access? Is the process efficient, effective, and timely? How could the process be improved?

8. How is student data secured in your school district? Are there any practices that concern you about privacy of student information? What might be done to address these concerns?

9. Examine the Acceptable Use Policy (AUP) for teachers and students in your district. Do you think it is complete and clear? What would you change about the AUP?

10. How can technology support the needs of culturally and linguistically diverse students in the classroom? To what extent are these strategies being implemented in your school? How can you help teachers use technology to implement culturally and linguistically responsive pedagogy?

11. To what extent is technology being used in your school to support cultural understanding, global awareness, and family/community involvement in students' education? How could these components be strengthened?

Essential Conditions Connection—ISTE Essential Conditions and ISTE Standards•C, Standard 5

When enacting Standard Five-Digital Citizenship, technology coaches support the following essential conditions:

- **Skilled Personnel**
- **Ongoing Professional Learning**
- **Assessment and Evaluation**

TABLE 5.3. ISTE Essential Conditions Related to ISTE Standards•C, 5

ISTE Essential Conditions	ISTE STANDARDS•C 5. Digital Citizenship
EQUITABLE ACCESS All students, teachers, staff, and school leaders have robust and reliable connectivity and access to current and emerging technologies and digital resources.	Digital Equity (ISTE Standards•C, 5a) Technology coaches advocate for the equitable access to digital tools and resources and technology-related best practices for all students and teachers.
SUPPORT POLICIES Policies, financial plans, accountability measures, and incentive structures support the use of ICT and other digital resources for both learning and district/school operations. **SUPPORTIVE EXTERNAL CONTEXT** Policies and initiatives at the national, regional, and local levels support schools and teacher preparation programs in the effective implementation of technology for achieving curriculum and learning technology/ ICT standards.	Safe, Healthy, Legal, and Ethical Uses (ISTE Standards•C, 5b) Digital Equity (ISTE Standards•C, 5a) Technology coaches understand the policies that are in place to support the implementation of technology, including those that promote the safe, healthy, legal, and ethical uses of technology and digital equity. Technology coaches help others understand and implement those policies, and they often contribute to policy development at the local, regional, and national levels.
ENGAGED COMMUNITIES Leaders and educators develop and maintain partnerships and collaboration within the community to support and fund the use of ICT and digital learning resources.	Diversity, Cultural Understanding, and Global Awareness (ISTE Standards•C, 5c) When technology coaches use digital age communication and collaboration tools to interact locally and globally with students, peers, parents, and the larger community, they contribute to engaged communities. When communities see the power of connected learning, technology coaches build support for digital age learning.

Resources for Digital Citizenship

DIGITAL EQUITY

U.S. Census Bureau Data

The U.S. Census Bureau collects information on computers and internet use from the entire U.S. population every 10 years and from a probability-selected sample of approximately 60,000 occupied households annually. Reports, data, and methodology can be found on these sites:

www.census.gov/hhes/computer/publications/2010.html

www.census.gov/hhes/computer/publications

Digital Divide Reports

In 2013, the Pew Research Center published a series of reports describing digital divides. Topics included access to internet, tablets, and mobile phones. A general report on how technology is used in schools and a specific report on how technology is influencing students' writing skills are also available. These reports can be accessed at

www.pewinternet.org/topics/digital-divide

One Laptop Per Child Initiative

One Laptop Per Child (OLPC) is a not-for-profit organization striving to equip the world's poorest children with durable, low-cost, mobile computing devices to support their education.

http://one.laptop.org

U.S. Federal E-Rate Program

The universal service Schools and Libraries Program, called the E-rate Program, helps all U.S. schools afford internet access and internal connections. It is an important program for supporting digital equity.

www.usac.org/sl

CoSN's Rethinking of Equity in a Digital Era Toolkit

The Consortium for School Networking has created a publication that encourages technology departments to partner with Title I directors to advance digital equity in U.S. schools. The report also outlines programs in Uruguay and Argentina as well as Portugal designed to address digital equity.

http://cosn.org/focus-areas/leadership-vision/digital-equity

http://cosn.org/digital-equity-toolkit

www.cosn.org/search/node/Digital%20Era%20Toolkit

DIGITAL CITIZENSHIP AND DIGITAL LITERACY

Several websites and books define digital citizenship and support digital literacy instruction. Mike Ribble's nine elements define digital citizenship and help educators identify what students should know and be able to do. The first URL below is a link to Ribble's website, where he discusses digital citizenship along with information on his two books. The other websites include curriculum materials from Common Sense Media, Canada's "Media Smarts" Centre for Digital and Media Literacy, and the Carnegie Cyber Academy. The digitalresponsibility.org site highlights useful information on digital citizenship topics and its Digital Responsibility Scholarships for high school, college, and graduate school students.

Websites

www.digitalcitizenship.net

www.iste.org/resources/searchresults?mediaType=bookwww.commonsensemedia.org/educators/curriculum

http://mediasmarts.ca/digital-media-literacy

www.carnegiecyberacademy.com/about.html

www.digitalresponsibility.org

Books

The following books offer concrete ideas for teaching digital literacy and digital citizenship.

Gura, M. (2014). *Teaching literacy in the digital age.* Eugene, OR: ISTE.

Ribble, M. (2015). *Digital citizenship in schools* (3rd ed.). Eugene, OR: ISTE.

INTERNET SAFETY AND CYBERBULLYING PREVENTION

Internet safety and cyberbullying prevention are important components of digital citizenship and digital literacy. In the United States, the Children's Internet Protection Act requires schools to educate students about internet safety. Many resources are dedicated to this important topic; tech coaches, teachers, students, and parents will find the websites and books listed here to be informative, reassuring, and practical.

Websites

www.connectsafely.org

www.netsmartz.org/Overview

www.ncpc.org/topics

http://ikeepsafe.org

www.safesurfingkids.com

https://safenet.3rox.net

www.fbi.gov/fun-games/kids/kids-safety

www.gcflearnfree.org/internetsafety

www.commonsensemedia.org/educators/connecting-families

www.whyville.net/smmk/nice

http://pbskids.org/webonauts

http://isafe.org/wp

http://cyberbullying.us

www.stopbullying.gov/cyberbullying

www.safekids.com

Books

Fodeman, D., & Monroe, M. (2013). *A parent's guide to online safety.* Eugene, OR: ISTE.

Fodeman, D., & Monroe, M. (2012). *Safe practices for life online: A guide for middle and high school* (2nd ed.). Eugene, OR: ISTE.

NETIQUETTE

Though appropriate internet communication etiquette, or *netiquette*, has been embedded into many digital citizenship resources, the following sites offer stand-alone information on this important topic:

Websites

www.learnthenet.com/index.php

www.albion.com/netiquette

www.carnegiecyberacademy.com/funStuff/netiquette/netiquette.html

www.networketiquette.net

ENVIRONMENTALLY FRIENDLY COMPUTING PRACTICES

Responsible computing requires practices that minimize harmful impacts on the environment and help ensure that children go to school in healthy surroundings. The following resources offer examples of environmentally responsible computing practices:

Websites

www.greenschools.net

www.cosn.org/GreenComputing

www.epa.gov/oaintrnt/practices/electronics.htm

HEALTHY COMPUTING

Too much computer use or using computers improperly can lead to serious health issues. Technology coaches must be aware of how to promote healthy computing in their schools.

The following list includes links on ergonomics from Apple and Microsoft, information on computer vision syndrome from the American Optometric Association, and links to health information from Digitalresponsibility.org and Healthy Computing for Kids.

Websites

www.apple.com/about/ergonomics

www.microsoft.com/hardware/en-us/support/healthy-computing-guide

www.microsoft.com/hardware/en-us/support/ergonomic-comfort

www.aoa.org/patients-and-public/caring-for-your-vision/protecting-your-vision/

computer-vision-syndrome?sso=y

www.digitalresponsibility.org/health-and-technology

www.healthycomputing.com/kids

PRIVACY AND SECURITY OF STUDENT DATA

Connected classrooms create new possibilities and some new dimensions for securing and protecting student information. Here are some publications on the topic of security and privacy in school settings:

Websites

Data in the Cloud: A Legal and Policy Guide for School Boards on Student Data Privacy in the Cloud Computing Era, National Association of School Boards (NASB), **www.nsba.org/sites/default/files/Data_In_The_Cloud_Guide_NSBA_COSA_02-09-15.pdf**

Digital Compliance and Student Privacy: A Roadmap for Schools, iKeepSafe, **http://ikeepsafe.org/educators_old/ digital-compliance-and-student-privacy-a-roadmap-for-schools**

PTAC Toolkit, Privacy Technical Assistance Center, U.S. Department of Education, **http://ptac.ed.gov/toolkit**

Protecting Privacy in Connected Learning: Considerations When Choosing an Online Service Provider for Your School System, Consortium for School Networking (CoSN), **www.cosn.org/sites/default/files/Privacy%20Toolkit_0319.pdf** and **www.cosn.org/ focus-areas/leadership-vision/protecting-privacy**

TEACHING ABOUT COPYRIGHT

Technology coaches must understand copyright principles themselves, help teachers understand what is lawful, and find ways for teachers to integrate copyright instruction into the curriculum. While copyright is a complex subject, there are ample resources to help educators and students understand and honor copyright law. Here are a few websites that contain a wealth of useful information:

Websites

www.copyrightfoundation.org/files/userfiles/file/EducatorsGuide.pdf

www.copyright.gov

www.teachingcopyright.org

www.copyrightkids.org

http://librarycopyright.net

http://wiki.wesfryer.com/t4t/resources/copyright

www.teachingchannel.org/videos/teaching-students-fair-use

www.teachingchannel.org/videos/teaching-students-copyright

www.commonsensemedia.org/videos/copyright-and-fair-use-animation

www.commonsensemedia.org/videos/teaching-kids-about-copyright-piracy

WEB ACCESSIBILITY

The following resources assist educators as they evaluate and create web content that is accessible to all learners:

National Center on Accessible Educational Materials (AEM), **http://aem.cast.org**

AEM Decision-Making Tools and Supports,
http://aem.cast.org/supporting/decision-tools.html#.VZ2TsmDVlis

WebAIM, **http://webaim.org**

WebAIM, Section 508 Checklist, **http://webaim.org/standards/508/checklist**

Web Accessibility Evaluation Tool (WAVE), **http://wave.webaim.org/**

Web Content Accessibility Guidelines (WCAG), **http://www.w3.org/WAI/intro/wcag**

CULTURALLY AND LINGUISTICALLY RESPONSIVE PEDAGOGY

To improve teachers' abilities to integrate technology into culturally and linguistically responsive pedagogy, technology coaches need to understand how to serve diverse learners. The following resources can help.

WIDA, which once stood for the World-class Instructional Design and Assessment organization, decided to drop its acronym definition and simply go by the letters WIDA; it publishes standards for English Language Learners (ELLs).

The What Works Clearinghouse identifies successful ELL instructional approaches; it is managed by the Institute for Education Sciences on behalf of the U.S. Department of Education.

Brown University's Culturally Responsive Teaching site summarizes and explains the importance of including students' cultural references in all aspects of learning, as defined by Gloria Ladson-Billings.

The books listed can help technology coaches better understand how to help teachers acknowledge students' original cultures and languages as part of their practices.

Websites

https://www.wida.us/standards

http://ies.ed.gov/ncee/wwc/Topic.aspx?sid=6

www.brown.edu/academics/education-alliance/teaching-diverse-learners/strategies-0/
culturally-responsive-teaching-0#ladson-billings

Books

Gay, G. (2010). *Culturally responsive teaching: Theory, research, and practice.* New York, NY: Teachers College Press.

Hill, J., & Miller, K. (2013). *Classroom instruction that works with English language learners* (2nd ed.). Alexandria, VA: ASCD.

Ladson-Billings, G. (2009). *The dreamkeepers: Successful teachers of African American students* (2nd ed.). San Francisco, CA; Jossey-Bass.

GLOBAL LEARNING

Connected classrooms make global collaborations possible for everyone. To get started, technology coaches and teachers can access practical online resources, such as the U.S. Department of Education's *Teacher's Guide to International Collaboration on the Internet* and a wealth of webinars, videos, and recordings of presentations from the 2015 Global Education Conference; archives of conferences from 2010 through 2014 contain even more valuable resources to scan! Reading the books listed here by educators experienced in global learning will add significantly to their depth of knowledge.

Websites

http://www2.ed.gov/teachers/how/tech/international/index.html

www.globaleducationconference.com

Books

Cavanaugh, T., & Burg, J. (2011). *Bookmapping: Lit trips and beyond.* Eugene, OR: ISTE.

Lindsay, J., & Davis, V. (2013). *Flattening classrooms, engaging minds: Move to global collaboration one step at a time.* Boston, MA: Pearson.

CHAPTER 6

Content Knowledge and Professional Growth

ISTE STANDARDS•C, STANDARD 6
Content Knowledge and Professional Growth

Technology coaches demonstrate professional knowledge, skills, and dispositions in content, pedagogical, and technological areas as well as adult learning and leadership and are continuously deepening their knowledge and expertise.

To meet the overarching ISTE Standards•C, Six, technology coaches must demonstrate that they can attend to *their own* learning. They must demonstrate the foundational knowledge, skills, and dispositions needed to perform their duties. They must also demonstrate that they can keep current in their field. Because the educational technology landscape changes quickly, technology coaches must be expert learners, continually embedding ongoing professional development into their own daily practice.

Thus, ISTE Standards•C, Six represents the depth, breadth, and complexity of what technology coaches must know and be able to do. As emphasized throughout all the standards, technology coaches need expertise in many different areas, including content, pedagogy, and technology. They also need advanced understandings in the fields of adult learning and leadership. Furthermore, this standard distinguishes among knowledge, skills, and dispositions. Technology coaches must have well-developed abilities in all three domains to transform schools into digital age learning environments.

Knowledge refers to the ability to understand and explain a specific concept, trend, or issue. Knowledge can be gleaned from studying theory, case studies, research, and best practices. It can also be constructed from one's own experiences and conversations with other professionals. While knowledge alone cannot effect change, it forms the basis for informed action.

Skills comprise the abilities to apply knowledge and expertise to perform tasks. Technology coaches must possess many skills, including designing professional learning programs, selecting and evaluating technologies, troubleshooting technological problems, and helping teachers adopt new practices. Accomplishing these tasks requires knowledge of and expertise in principles, processes, procedures, and strategies. While knowledge can help technology coaches identify these components, coaches must have perfected the necessary skills to model and teach them to others.

Dispositions refer to beliefs, values, attitudes, and effective ways of interacting with others. Dispositions are important because they affect how knowledge and skills are enacted. For example, technology coaches may have great knowledge and skills in constructivist learning, but if they do not believe that this instructional approach is good for students, they will not promote it. Similarly, if technology coaches are unable to build strong, trusting relationships with others, they will not be effective change agents.

The overarching concepts apply to three elements in ISTE Standards•C, Standard Six. These elements describe what technology coaches must know and be able to do to deepen and demonstrate their content knowledge and professional growth:

- Content, Pedagogical, and Technical Knowledge

- Professional Knowledge, Skills, and Dispositions

- Self-Evaluation and Reflection

Content, Pedagogical, and Technical Knowledge

ISTE STANDARDS•C, 6a

Content, Pedagogical, and Technical Knowledge

Engage in continual learning to deepen content and pedagogical knowledge in technology integration and current and emerging technologies necessary to effectively implement the Standards•S and Standards•T.

ISTE Standards•C, 6a is influenced by an accepted framework for understanding what teachers must know and be able to do to integrate technology into teaching, called Technological Pedagogical Content Knowledge (TPACK, formerly TPCK). Punya Mishra and Matthew J. Koehler are known for their work on TPACK, which extends Lee S. Shulman's idea of pedagogical content knowledge. As discussed in Chapter Two, teachers need much more than technology training to use technology successfully in their classrooms. They also need to understand how technology can support students' acquisition of content knowledge and how tech can support their own successful teaching practices or pedagogy. As illustrated in Figure 6.1, expert digital age teachers must possess an advanced understanding of how they can combine technology, pedagogy, and content to create powerful learning environments for students.

Because technology coaches help teachers design these environments, the TPACK framework can also be used to describe what technology coaches need to know and be able to do to promote successful technology integration. In short, technology coaches must develop their own technological, pedagogical, and content knowledge in order to help teachers do the same.

According to ISTE Standards•C, 6a, technology coaches should seek the content, pedagogical, and technological knowledge necessary to implement the Standards for Teachers (ISTE Standards•T) and Students (ISTE Standards•S). The ISTE Standards•T and Standards•S represent what teachers and students should know in a digital age world. These standards clearly promote student-centered learning, higher-order thinking, problem-solving, creativity, and innovation in digital age classrooms. When technology coaches are developing their content, pedagogical, and technological, skills to implement Standards•S and Standards•T, they are achieving ISTE Standards•C, 6a.

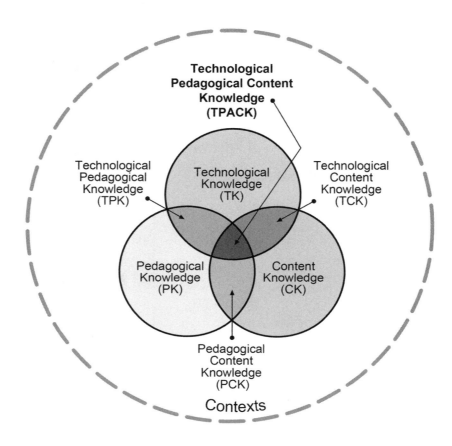

FIGURE 6.1. TPACK Diagram (reproduced by permission of the publisher, © 2012 by tpack.org)

For more detailed information on TPACK, see the following resources:

RESOURCES ON TPACK

www.tpack.org

Koehler, M. J., & Mishra, P. (2008). Introducing TPCK. *In Handbook of technological peda-gogical content knowledge (TPCK) for educators*, pp. 3–29. Edited by the Committee on Innovation and Technology, American Association of Colleges of Teacher Education. New York, NY: AACTE and Routledge.

Koehler, M. J., Mishra, P., Bouck, E., DeSchryver, M., Kereluik, K., Shin, T. S., & Wolf, L. G. (2011). Deep-play: Developing TPACK for 21st century teachers. *International Journal of Learning Technology 6*(2), 146–163.

Koehler, M. J., Mishra, P., Kereluik, K., Shin, T. S., & Graham, C. R. (2014). The technological pedagogical content knowledge framework. In *Handbook of research on educational com-munications and technology*, pp. 101–111. Edited by J. M. Specter, M. D. Merrill, J. Elen, & M. J. Bishop. New York, NY: Springer.

Professional Knowledge, Skills, and Dispositions

ISTE STANDARDS•C, 6b
Professional Knowledge, Skills, and Dispositions

Engage in continuous learning to deepen professional knowledge, skills, and dispositions in organizational change and leadership, project management, and adult learning to improve professional practice.

Technology coaches have numerous roles and responsibilities. They are educators who must develop their own TPACK frameworks. They are also expected to be exemplary educational leaders, change agents, professional development experts, community liaisons, web masters, grant writers, evaluators, and technologists. To excel, tech coaches need to employ profes-sional knowledge from a wide variety of disciplines, including but not necessarily limited to organizational change, leadership, project management, and adult learning.

Acquiring information from such a wide range of sources can seem daunting; however, tech coaches can acquire knowledge over time and on an as-needed basis. The keys to successful multidisciplinary learning are to scan broadly and to be familiar with a few good resources in critical, related knowledge domains. Building a social network of people with diverse areas of expertise is another effective strategy for keeping informed and up to date. As tech-nology coaches define themselves more broadly and gain expertise in more disciplines, they will be able to promote technology-supported learning in new ways.

TECHNOLOGY COACHING CASE STUDY

Organizing Every Moment for Maximized Learning

—Anthony St. Jean

Technology Coordinator
HEYWOOD AVENUE SCHOOL, GRADES PK–7
ORANGE PUBLIC SCHOOLS, ORANGE, NEW JERSEY

ISTE STANDARDS•C, 6a: Engage in continual learning to deepen content and pedagogical knowledge in technology integration and current and emerging technologies necessary to effectively implement the Standards•S and Standards•T.

ISTE STANDARDS•C 6b: Engage in continuous learning to deepen professional knowledge, skills, and dispositions in organizational change and leadership, project management, and adult learning to improve professional practice.

On weekdays and weekends, Anthony St. Jean gets up very early in the mornings when his house is quiet and slips to his computer. His favorite webpages are bookmarked, and he uses Feedly to aggregate sites with RSS, so it doesn't take him very long to scan the day's educational technology news. He also checks into his Facebook and Twitter accounts to see what other educational technologists are posting.

When it's time to go to work, Bluetooth technology allows St. Jean to listen to educational technology podcasts through his car's audio system. He also enjoys listening to audio books on education-related topics, such as leadership and technology trends.

At work, he learns from doing and learns from his colleagues, but contact with outside material is limited to an occasional, quick web search or an exchange in a discussion forum to solve a specific problem. Mostly, he uses online technical forums and social network sites sponsored by ISTE and by the New Jersey Association for Educational Technology, where he can post questions and receive timely responses.

On the evening commute, he plugs in again for more podcasts and audio books. Most nights, he spends a few minutes reading online resources before turning in.

Once a year, he attends New Jersey's Educational Technology Conference and ISTE's Conference & Expo. He finds that attending sessions and volunteering expand his social learning networks and help him identify topics for further study when he comes back home.

"It may sound time-consuming to keep up, and I guess it is, but it's fun! I love to learn, and I want to know these things. I'd do my job for free if I could. My advice to tech coaches is to keep things simple. Do a few things well, rather than many things halfheartedly," he concluded.

For more information about St. Jean's district and school, visit: **www.orange.k12.nj.us** and **www.orange.k12.nj.us/heywood/site/default.asp**

Self-Evaluation and Reflection

ISTE STANDARDS•C, 6c

Self-Evaluation and Reflection

Regularly evaluate and reflect on their professional practice and dispositions to improve and strengthen their abilities to effectively model and facilitate technology-enhanced learning experiences.

Given the pace of their work, it might sound impossible for technology coaches to regularly evaluate and reflect on their knowledge, skills, dispositions, and performances. Yet, this is exactly what ISTE Standards • C, 6c asks technology coaches to do.

Reflection is a special way of thinking about past events for the purposes of future improvement. Many emphasize the role of experience in the professional learning process. Yet, experience alone really is not enough to promote powerful learning. Experts agree that learning actually occurs when individuals reflect on their experiences. Reflective and evaluative thought processes focus on answering questions such as these:

- What worked?

- What didn't work?

- Why?

- What would work better next time?

Though reflection is frequently portrayed as a solitary activity, reflection with others is also recommended. Teachers, students, and other technology coaches can provide feedback about performances and help each other generate ideas for future activities. All effective personal, professional development plans need to include self-evaluation and reflection on how to improve performances.

TECHNOLOGY COACHING CASE STUDY

Coaches Never Stop Learning

—Jill Brown

Director of Educational Technology and Technology Coach
ALBUQUERQUE ACADEMY
ALBUQUERQUE, NEW MEXICO

ISTE STANDARDS•C, Standard 6: Content Knowledge and Professional GrowthTechnology coaches demonstrate professional knowledge, skills, and dispositions in content, pedagogical, and technological areas as well as adult learning and leadership and are continuously deepening their knowledge and expertise.

ISTE STANDARDS•C, 6a: Engage in continual learning to deepen content and pedagogical knowledge in technology integration and current and emerging technologies necessary to effectively implement the Standards•S and Standards•T.

ISTE STANDARDS•C, 6b: Engage in continuous learning to deepen professional knowledge, skills, and dispositions in organizational change and leadership, project management, and adult learning to improve professional practice.

Even though Jill Brown is a director of educational technology, she still spends between 60 to 70% of her time coaching teachers.

"I believe the ISTE Standards•C are important prerequisites for the ISTE Standards for Technology Directors. I am a better technology director because I was a coach first, and I didn't stop coaching when I became a director. The combined coach/director roles are especially common in smaller school systems," states Brown.

Brown believes that a combination of formal education, ongoing professional learning, and on-the-job experience prepared her to be a good coach. Brown points to her undergraduate degree and teaching experience in elementary education as a critical foundation for her coaching practices. Her work toward earning a master's degree and a doctorate in curriculum and instruction and educational technology helped her understand how children, adolescents, and adults learn.

Brown attributes most of her technology expertise to self-study and ongoing professional development. Since technologies change all the time, she tinkers with different products on a day-to-day basis and evaluates their usefulness for K–12 settings. Professional organizations, such as ISTE and the New Mexico Society for Technology in Education, keep her up-to-date on emerging technologies and technology-related issues in schools. She attends conferences, workshops, and webinars. To stay connected to a network of peers, Brown volunteers for committees and participates in online professional communities, such as the ISTE Profressional Learning Networks (PLNs).

Overall, Brown characterizes professional learning for technology coaches as invigorating and challenging: "We are technology experts but also education experts. That means we have to draw from a broad knowledge base. We have to constantly learn, but that's what makes it exciting and why people really need us to help them."

Performance in Content Knowledge and Professional Growth

The ISTE Technology Coaching Rubric describes performances that approach, meet, and exceed expectations for ISTE Standards • C, Standard Six: Content Knowledge and Professional Growth. This section is designed to provide an explanation of the rubric as related to Standard Six and to provide more examples in each category.

Table 6.2 illustrates how technology coaches can continue to improve their content knowledge and professional growth. Note the differences in performances among the approaches, meets, and exceeds levels.

ISTE Standards • C, Standard Six is slightly different from the other five Standards • C standards. Standard Six is focused on technology coaches' professional learning needs.

TABLE 6.2. Technology Coaching Rubric for Standard 6

Standard 6. Content Knowledge and Professional Growth

Technology coaches demonstrate professional knowledge, skills, and dispositions in content, pedagogical, and technological areas as well as adult learning and leadership and are continuously deepening their knowledge and expertise.

a. **Content, Pedagogical, and Technical Knowledge.** Engage in continual learning to deepen content and pedagogical knowledge in technology integration and current and emerging technologies necessary to effectively implement the Standards•S and Standards•T.

b. **Professional Knowledge.** Engage in continuous learning to deepen professional knowledge, skills, and dispositions in organizational change and leadership, project management, and adult learning to improve professional practice.

c. **Reflection.** Regularly evaluate and reflect on their professional practice and dispositions to improve and strengthen their abilities to effectively model and facilitate technology-enhanced learning experiences.

Approaches	Meets	Exceeds
TECHNOLOGY COACHES: • identify foundational principles related to content and pedagogical knowledge in technology integration and current and emerging technologies necessary to effectively implement the Standards•S and Standards•T. (6a) • identify basic foundational principles related to organizational change and leadership, project management, and adult learning to improve professional practice. (6b) • identify qualities and best practices of a reflective practitioner and understand why self-evaluation/reflection is beneficial. (6c) • identify strategies to engage in continuous learning, evaluation, and reflection to deepen content knowledge and professional growth related to content and pedagogical knowledge, emerging technologies, technology integration, technology standards, organizational change, leadership, project management, and adult learning. (6a–c)	TECHNOLOGY COACHES: • engage in continual learning to deepen content and pedagogical knowledge in technology integration and current and emerging technologies necessary to effectively implement the Standards•S and Standards•T. (6a) • engage in continuous learning to deepen professional knowledge, skills, and dispositions in organizational change and leadership, project management, and adult learning to improve professional practice. (6b) • regularly evaluate and reflect on their professional practice and dispositions to improve and strengthen their ability to effectively model and facilitate technology-enhanced learning experiences. (6c)	TECHNOLOGY COACHES: • produce resources or engage in professional activities that assist others in developing their knowledge of content and pedagogy, emerging technologies, technology integration, technology standards, organizational change, leadership, project management, and/or adult learning. (6a–b) • produce resources or engage in professional activities that assist others in evaluating their own professional practices and/or dispositions to improve and strengthen their abilities to effectively model and facilitate technology-enhanced learning experiences. (6c) • provide evidence that these resources or professional activities have contributed to the professional growth of other technology coaches or educational leaders responsible for supporting effective technology implementation. (6a–c)

In the previous five chapters, we have discussed ISTE Standards • C, Standards One through Five. Standards One through Five emphasize helping other educators implement technology in their classrooms or workplaces. However, Standards • C, Standard Six is about content knowledge and professional learning. When technology coaches advance their own knowledge, skills, and dispositions, technically they can meet Standard Six. Of course, the fundamental reason for coaches to improve and perfect these understandings and skills is to help their colleagues.

Not all professional learning activities qualify as meeting ISTE Standards•C, Standard Six. In Figure 6.2, consider the first two bullet points in the Approaches and Meets columns: the rubric distinguishes between being able to *identify* the basic foundational principles needed to enter the technology coaching profession (approaches) and being able to *engage in* continual learning (meets). To fully meet ISTE Standards•C, 6a and 6b, technology coaches must show that they have mastered the basics for entering the field—as defined by meeting ISTE Standards•C, Standards 1–5, and to fully meet Standards•C, 6c, they must know how to continually advance their professional knowledge, skills, and dispositions.

As with many other ISTE Standards•C standards, the *exceeds* column for the Standard 6 ISTE Technology Coaching Rubric requires *assisting others*, but the exceeding performances for this standard are quite different from their counterparts. The *exceeds* column must be read in the overarching context of ISTE Standards•C, Standard 6, which relates to the professional knowledge, skills, and dispositions needed to help others implement technology. Therefore, exceeding performances require helping others to engage in technology coaching, not simply changing their own classroom practices. To exceed expectations for Standard 6, technology coaches must help others do the work that they are doing themselves.

APPROACHES

Sandra is a brand new, part-time technology coach. Other than using technology in her own classroom, she has had little preparation for her new job. To learn about the professional resources available to technology coaches, she searches the internet for resources. She finds several websites, and her principal gives her the ISTE Standards for Technology Coaches (ISTE Standards•C).

Kerry is a teacher who aspires to be a full-time technology coach. To help him prepare for this position, he entered an instructional technology master's program based on the ISTE Standards•C standards. During the first two semesters of the program, he has taken classes related to technology leadership, professional learning, internet tools, and digital citizenship. Kerry has learned basic principles related to organizational change, adult learning, technology integration, and internet safety.

Joseph is an experienced technology coach. His district is implementing a new personnel evaluation approach that requires Joseph to write personal learning goals, engage in reflection, and provide evidence of professional growth. While this process is new to him, he is enjoying attending professional development training on the art of reflection and how it can improve his practice. Joseph is also reading books and articles related to professional reflection.

Justine has been a technology coach for six months. She likes her job and is surprised that she has to attend many meetings about district-level projects. Since she sometimes feels a little lost at these meetings, she has asked her principal and the district technology director how she can improve her knowledge. The principal and the technology director have given Justine some background on the district's technology journey and have suggested some educational leadership resources to help her.

MEETS

Stuart has been a high school technology coach for five years. He enjoys keeping up-to-date on emerging technologies and sharing new products with teachers at his school. He uses Twitter, several websites, and magazines to look for promising resources and shares information with teachers via an e-newsletter he publishes each Friday. He highlights how teachers can use new tech tools to teach the required curriculum. Stuart archives the resources he's mentioned in the newsletter on his own website; when the teachers are ready to try them, they can find the information easily.

Kelvin has been a technology coach for 15 years. He keeps up with educational technology journals, magazines, websites, and conferences and enjoys going to his school library and scanning the literature related to educational leadership and curriculum planning. He also frequents the local bookstore to read technical magazines learn about new resources. Right now, he is reading a book from the business sector on managing technology projects and applying what he is learning to the BYOD initiative he is managing at his own school.

Sydney has served as a full-time technology coach for eight elementary and middle schools in her large district over the past six years. Given her busy schedule, it would seem that reflection on her own practice would be impossible, but she says that reflection is what keeps her organized and energized. She journals daily and keeps a log of her coaching activities. Each Friday, Sydney and the other nine district technology coaches meet to compare notes. If they have a difficult case or situation, they brainstorm for possible strategies. In addition to helping each other with their personal goals, the team analyzes evaluation data from district-level projects. Studying the evaluation results helps them come up with ideas for making the changes necessary to meet goals for district initiatives.

EXCEEDS

Malcolm works with a team of 10 other technology coaches in his district. They all enjoy sharing instructional technology resources and learning from one another. Malcolm, an active and enthusiastic learner, almost always has found something new to show his colleagues at their department meetings. He also frequently shares articles and resources with his building's principals. Malcolm has written several articles on the art of technology coaching, and many technology coaches throughout the country call on him for advice.

Deborah, a new technology coach three years ago, found the ISTE Standards • C and rubric very helpful. When Deborah learned that her district was going to hire two new technology coaches, she used the ISTE Standards • C and rubric to craft possible interview questions Her district technology director liked Deborah's questions so much that the team used all of them in the interview process. A few months later, Deborah shared the same interview questions with colleagues at a state educational technology conference. Several districts' tech directors emailed Deborah to thank her, saying that they had used her questions to hire highly qualified technology coaches.

Nucheki thought she would work exclusively with teachers when she was hired to be a technology coach. However, over the years, she realized that helping principals become good technology coaches was also an important component of her job. She began conducting ed techn updates for the principals, including best practices in instructional technology and articles on trends and issues. Her principals appreciated Nucheki's updates so much that she decided to start publishing the material in the updates online. Now, more than 100,000 subscribers follow her Twitter feed, and she is regularly invited to speak to principals at conferences.

Discussion Questions for Content Knowledge and Professional Growth

1. How helpful is TPACK in describing what technology coaches must know and be able to do? What level of technical, pedagogical, and content knowledge do you currently possess? Which areas do you want to strengthen and why? How will you improve your knowledge and skills?

2. How do you keep up-to-date in the field of instructional technology? What are your favorite learning resources and strategies? What new professional learning goals do you want to pursue in the future?

3. Do you believe professional reflection is useful? Why or why not? What are some ways to engage in professional reflection? How could you strengthen reflective activities in your own practice?

Essential Conditions Connection—ISTE Essential Conditions and ISTE Standards•C, Standard 6

When addressing Standard Six–Content Knowledge and Professional Growth, technology coaches support the following essential conditions:

- **Skilled Personnel**

- **Ongoing Professional Learning**

TABLE 6.3. ISTE Essential Conditions Related to ISTE Standards•C, 6

ISTE Essential Conditions	ISTE STANDARDS•C 6. Content Knowledge and Professional Growth
SKILLED PERSONNEL Educators, support staff, and other leaders are skilled in the selection and effective use of appropriate ICT resources. ONGOING PROFESSIONAL LEARNING Educators have ongoing access to technology-related professional learning plans and opportunities as well as dedicated time to practice and share ideas.	Content, Pedagogical, and Technical Knowledge (ISTE Standards•C, 6a) Professional Knowledge (ISTE Standards•C, 6b) Reflection (ISTE Standards•C, 6c) When addressing ISTE Standards•C, Standard Six, technology coaches care for their own professional learning and advance their own knowledge and skills. In doing so, they strengthen ISTE's essential conditions for skilled personnel and ongoing professional learning. By being the best they can be, technology coaches are better equipped to help others.

Resources for Content Knowledge and Professional Growth

PROFESSIONAL ORGANIZATIONS FOR EDUCATIONAL TECHNOLOGY

International Society for Technology in Education (ISTE)

ISTE serves more than 100,000 education stakeholders around the world. ISTE hosts an annual Conference & Expo with approximately 20,000 participants, 1,000 concurrent sessions, and 500 exhibits.

Dedicated to advancing the use of technology to improve teaching and learning, the organization publishes a quarterly magazine, books and peer-reviewed journals and publications; hosts social learning communities for educators; and produces a daily blog on tech tips, trends, and leaders; webinars and podcasts; an online self-assessment tool for educators, and a professional learning program. ISTE's membership includes technology coordinators, technology directors, teachers, university faculty, administrators, and library/media specialists.

www.iste.org

http://conference.iste.org/2016

www.iste.org/docs/news-documents/iste-press-kit.pdf?sfvrsn=2

ISTE Affiliates and Conferences

ISTE partners with a network of organizations that share their vision. These organizations provide additional professional development opportunities for educators in their states, regions, or countries, including state and regional conferences. ISTE's website includes links to all affiliates, including organizations in Canada, Europe, India, Australia, and the Philippines.

http://www.iste.org/lead/affiliate-directory

Consortium for School Networking (CoSN)

CoSN is a professional organization that supports district-level technology leaders. It publishes resources on infrastructure and policies targeted to the needs of technology directors, including *The Framework of Essential Skills of the K-12 CTO* (chief Technology officer). The organization also administers the Certified Education Technology Leader (CETL) exam.

www.cosn.org

www.cosn.org/Framework

National School Board Association (NSBA), Technology Leadership Network (TLN)

The NSBA's TLN serves school board members, administrators, and district technology personnel to help them make well-informed technology decisions. The TLN produces white papers and other brief publications, sponsors an annual conference, and hosts site visits to districts with exemplary technology programs.

www.nsba.org/services/technology-leadership-network www.nsba.org/services/technology-leadership-network/how-join-tln

Association for the Advancement of Computing in Education (AACE)

AACE strives to advance information technology in education and e-learning. The organization focuses on research, development, and the practical applications of learning technologies. It sponsors four annual conferences and produces peer-reviewed journals and publications.

www.aace.org

Association for Educational Communications and Technology (AECT)

AECT is a professional association serving those who want to improve instruction through technology. AECT members include higher education faculty and staff; military personnel; and employees of corporations, small businesses, museums, libraries, and hospitals. The organization's *Handbook for Research of Educational Communications and Technology* (4th ed.)) is a resource for professors, graduate students,

www.aect.org/newsite

State Educational Technology Directors Association (SETDA)

SETDA serves state-level educational directors in the United States. Although these directors are usually employed by state departments of education, SETDA publications and reports are also beneficial for school and district-level technology leaders.

www.setda.org/about/

OTHER SCHOOL LEADERSHIP ORGANIZATIONS

American Association of School Librarians (AASL)

School library media personnel share a mission with all educators to advance educational technology for teaching and learning. Valuable information is available in AASL journals, and other publications; at its conferences; and through its online learning and continuing education programs.

http://www.ala.org/aasl/

ASCD, a professional organization serving curriculum directors, principals, and other school leaders, focuses on helping leaders provide high-quality instruction. Technology coaches can benefit from following this organization's conferences; its publications, including the daily SmartBrief; and professional development programs to better understand instructional research, trends, and initiatives.

www.ascd.org

Learning Forward (formerly the National Staff Development Council)

Learning Forward is a professional organization dedicated to supporting high-quality professional development. It publishes standards for professional learning and other resources for professional development providers.

http://learningforward.org

National Association of Elementary and Secondary School Principals (NAESP, NASSP)

Since technology coaches work closely with principals, updates and publications from NAESP and NASSP can often be beneficial to coaches. These organizations also help highlight important trends and issues in U.S. schools.

www.naesp.org

www.nassp.org

CONTENT AREA PROFESSIONAL ORGANIZATIONS

Technology coaches can subscribe to updates and scan resources from the following professional organizations to build TPACK and other knowledge related to professional growth in the disciplines they support.

American Council on the Teaching of Foreign Languages (ACTFL), **www.actfl.org**

Computer Science Teachers Association (CSTA), **http://csta.acm.org**

Music Teachers National Association (MTNA), **www.mtna.org**

National Art Education Association (NAEA), **www.arteducators.org**

National Association of Special Education Teachers (NASET), **www.naset.org**

National Council of Teachers of English (NCTE), **www.ncte.org**

National Council of Teachers of Mathematics **(NCTM), www.nctm.org**

National Council for the Social Studies, **www.socialstudies.org**

National Science Teachers Association, **www.nsta.org**

Society of Health and Physical Educators (SHAPE America), **www.shapeamerica.org**

Teachers of English to Speakers of Other Languages (TESOL) International Organization **www.tesol.org**

SCIENCE, TECHNOLOGY, ENGINEERING, AND MATH (STEM) RESOURCES

Given the emphasis on STEM education, technology coaches can keep up-to-date on STEM initiatives and funding opportunities through the following resources:

The National Science Foundation (NSF)

The NSF is U.S. government agency charged with promoting the progress of science. Its website highlights new scientific and funding opportunities.

www.nsf.gov

STEM Education Coalition

The STEM Education Coalition is an advocacy group that promotes high-quality STEM initiatives to key policy makers. The coalition's website chronicles key developments in STEM education programs.

www.stemedcoalition.org

STEMconnector

STEMconnector is a not-for-profit organization that hosts a website and produces STEM daily updates useful for gathering STEM resources.

www.stemconnector.org

Code.org

Code.org is a not-for-profit organization that helps educators integrate computer science into their curriculums. Its Hour of Code program has made a global impact on elementary and secondary students.

http://code.org

GOVERNMENT EDUCATION AGENCIES

Most countries have education agencies at the national and state levels. Some of them also have divisions related to educational technology. A few are listed as examples:

United States Department of Education, Office of Educational Technology, **http://tech.ed.gov**

Links to U.S. state departments of education, commonwealths, and territories **/www2.ed.gov/about/contacts/state/index.html**

Australian Government Department of Education and Training, **https://education.gov.au**

Ministries/Departments responsible for education in Canada, **http://www.cicic.ca/1301/Ministries-Departments-responsible-for-education-in-Canada/index.canada**

PRACTITIONER JOURNALS, NEWSPAPERS, MAGAZINES, AND WEBSITES

The following is a list of popular practitioner resources that technology coaches and other educational leaders read regularly. They provide up-to-date info on new products, trends, policies, issues, and success stories from schools.

Education Week, **www.edweek.org/ew/index.html**

eSchool News, **www.eschoolnews.com**

entrsekt, published by ISTE, **www.iste.org/explore/entrsekt**

TechTrends (formerly Tech Trends for Leaders in Education and Training), published by the Association for Educational Communications & Technology (AECT) **http://link.springer.com/journal/11528**

THE Journal: Technological Horizons in Education, **http://thejournal.com**

Tech & Learning, **www.techlearning.com**

EDUCATIONAL TECHNOLOGY JOURNALS

The following peer-reviewed, academic journals publish research on instructional technology topics. Most of these journals can be accessed through a school library with academic databases. Those available online at no cost are noted.

American Journal of Distance Education (AJDE) **www.tandfonline.com/loi/hajd20#.VaWH8WDVlis**

Australasian Journal of Educational Technology (AJET), published by the Australasian Society for

Computers in Learning in Tertiary Education (ASCILITE)
http://ascilite.org.au/ajet/

British Journal of Educational Technology (BJET), **http://eu.wiley.com/WileyCDA/WileyTitle/productCd-BJET.html**

Computers & Education, **www.sciencedirect.com/science/journal/03601315**

Contemporary Issues in Technology & Teacher Education (the CITE Journal),published by the Society for Information Technology and Teacher Education (SITE), was established as a multimedia, interactive counterpart of the Journal of Technology and Teacher Education. SITE operates under the auspices of the Association for the Advancement of Computing in Education (AACE). The CITE Journal is jointly sponsored by the AMTE, ASTE, NCSS-CUFA, CEE, and SITE. (Free Online Journal) **www.citejournal.org**

Journal of Educational Technology & Society (JET&S), published by the International Forum of Educational Technology & Society, **www.ifets.info**

Educational Technology Research & Development (ETR&D), published by the Association for Educational Communications & Technology (AECT) **www.springer.com/education+%26+language/learning+%26+instruction/journal/11423**

International Journal of Computer-Supported Collaborative Learning (ijCSL), published by the International Society of the Learning Sciences, **http://ijcscl.org**

International Journal on E-Learning (IJEL), published by Association for the Advancement of Computing in Education (AACE), **www.editlib.org/j/IJEL**

The International Review of Research in Open and Distributed Learning (IRRODL) published by Athabasca University Press (Free Online Journal), **www.irrodl.org/index.php/irrodl/index**

The Internet and Higher Education (IHE), published by Elsevier **www.journals.elsevier.com/the-internet-and-higher-education**

Journal of Computer Assisted Learning (JCAL), published by John Wiley & Sons **http://onlinelibrary.wiley.com/journal/10.1111(ISSN)1365-2729**

Journal of Computers in Mathematics and Science Teaching (JCMST), published by the Association for the Advancement of Computing in Education (AACE), **http://www.editlib.org/j/JCMST/**

Journal of Digital Learning in Teacher Education (JDLTE), published by the International Society for Technology in Education (ISTE), **www.iste.org/learn/publications/journals/jdlte**

Journal of Educational Multimedia and Hypermedia (JEMH), published by Association for the Advancement of Computing in Education (AACE), **www.editlib.org/j/JEMH**

Journal of Interactive Learning Research (JILR), published by the Association for the Advancement of Computing in Education (AACE), **www.editlib.org/j/JILR**

Journal of Research on Technology in Education (JRTE), published by the International Society for Technology in Education (ISTE), **www.iste.org/learn/publications/journals/jrte**

Journal of Technology and Teacher Education (JTATE), published by the Society for Information Technology & Teacher Education (SITE), under the auspices of the Association for the Advancement of Computing in Education (AACE), **www.editlib.org/j/JTATE**

International Journal of K–12 Online and Blended Learning (IJKOBL), published by Open Journal Systems, the Public Knowledge Project (**http://pkp.sfu.ca**), (Free Online Journal) **www.ijkobl.com/index.php?journal=ijkobl**

Journal for Multicultural Education (formerly Multicultural Education & Technology Journal, published by Emerald Group, **www.emeraldinsight.com/loi/jme**

Tech Trends, published by the Association for Educational Communications and Technology (AECT), under the auspices of Springer
www.springer.com/education+%26+language/learning+%26+instruction/journal/11528

The Journal of Literacy and Technology (JLT), (Free Online Journal)
www.literacyandtechnology.org

OTHER USEFUL PEER-REVIEWED JOURNALS

To be respected as fellow educators, not only as the wizards who understand the mysteries of how computers and the internet work, we need to keep up with general educational trends. And to excel as coaches, we absolutely must be able to help our colleagues locate specific research in all disciplines—usually with little or no advance warning!

The following peer-reviewed, academic journals are not directly related to instructional technology, yet technology-related topics frequently appear in them. As tech coaches, we need to remind ourselves to stay abreast of nontechnology content. I highly recommend the American Educational Research Journal to tech coaches for regular reading. These resources, as well as all the others mentioned in this book, can be accessed through school library databases. A few are available online at no cost.

American Educational Research Journal (AERJ), published by the American Education Research Association (AERA) and Sage, **http://aer.sagepub.com**

American Journal of Distance Education (AJDE), published by Taylor & Francis
www.tandfonline.com/toc/hajd20/current#.VagSbGDVlis

Computer Assisted Language Learning, published by Taylor & Francis
www.tandfonline.com/loi/ncal20#.VagS-mDVlis

Distance Education, published by Open and Distance Learning Association of Australia (ODLAA) and Taylor and Francis
www.tandfonline.com/toc/cdie20/current#.VagTpmDVlit

Interactive Learning Environments, published by Taylor & Francis
www.tandfonline.com/toc/nile20/current#.VagYBWDVliu

International Journal of Education in Mathematics, Science and Technology (IJEMST)
http://ijemst.com/home.html

International Journal of Science and Mathematics Education (IJSME), published by the Ministry of Science and Technology, Taiwan, and Springer
www.springer.com/education+%26+language/mathematics+education/journal/10763

International Review of Research in Open and Distance Learning (IRRODL), published by the International Council for Open and Distance Education and the Canadian Institute of Distance Education Research at Athabasca University
www.icde.org/International+Review+of+Research+in+Open+and+Distance+Learning.9U FRvQ2V.ips

Journal of Early Childhood Research, published by Sage
http://ecr.sagepub.com

Journal of Early Childhood Literacy, published by Sage
http://ecl.sagepub.com

Journal of Early Childhood Teacher Education, published by the National Association of Early Childhood Teacher Educators and Taylor & Francis
www.tandfonline.com/loi/ujec20/current#

Journal of Educational Computing Research, published by Sage, **https://us.sagepub.com/en-us/nam/journal-of-educational-computing-research/journal202399**

Journal of Interactive Learning Research (JILR), published by the Association for the Advancement of Computers in Education (AACE), **www.aace.org/pubs/jilr**

Journal for Research in Mathematics Education, published by the National Council of Teachers of Mathematics (NCTM)
www.nctm.org/publications/journal-for-research-in-mathematics-education

Journal of Online Learning Research (JOLR), published by the Association for the Advancement of Computers in Education (AACE) and distributed by EdITLib, (Free Online Journal)
www.aace.org/pubs/jolr

Journal of Science Education and Technology, published by Springer
www.springer.com/education+%26+language/science+education/journal/10956

Journal of Research in Science Teaching (JRST), published by Wiley
http://onlinelibrary.wiley.com/journal/10.1002/%28ISSN%291098-2736

The Journal of Special Education (SED), published by the Hammill Institute on Disabilities and Sage
http://sed.sagepub.com

Journal of Special Education Technology (JSET), published by the Council for Exceptional Children, published by the Technology and Media Division of the Council for Exceptional Children
www.tamcec.org/jset

Language Learning & Technology (LLT), published by the National Foreign Language Resource Center at the University of Hawaii, the University of Hawai'i Center for Language and Technology, and the Center for Language Education and Research at Michigan State University
http://llt.msu.edu

Learning, Media and Technology, published by Taylor & Francis
www.tandfonline.com/toc/cjem20/current#

Reading Research Quarterly (RRQ), published by the International Literacy Association (formerly the International Reading Association) and Wiley
http://onlinelibrary.wiley.com/journal/10.1002/(ISSN)1936-2722

Research in the Teaching of English (RTE), published by National Council of Teachers of English (NCTE)
www.ncte.org/journals/rte

Review of Educational Research (RER), published by the American Educational Research Association (AERA) and Sage
http://rer.sagepub.com

The Journal of Social Studies Research (JSSR), published by the International Society for the Social Studies and Elsevier
www.journals.elsevier.com/the-journal-of-social-studies-research

The Turkish Online Journal of Educational Technology (TOJET), sponsored by Sakarya University and Manhattanville College and affiliated with the Association for Educational Communication & Technology
www.tojet.net/

TESOL Quarterly, published by the TESOL International Association and Wiley
http://onlinelibrary.wiley.com/journal/10.1002/%28ISSN%291545-7249/homepage/Contact.html

CONCLUSION

Summary and Next Steps

By exploring the ISTE Standards for Technology Coaches (ISTE Standards • C), this book has provided an in-depth look at what technology coaches should know and be able to do to support the effective use of technology in the classroom. On one level, the ISTE Standards • C help aspiring technology coaches to prepare for the future and prompt practicing technology coaches to sharpen or expand their current performance. On a broader scale, the standards shape the personal, professional identities of technology coaches and validate their contributions to the larger community.

The ISTE Standards • C clearly portray technology coaches as indispensible educational leaders in school improvement and enhanced student learning. As the standards illustrate, technology coaches contribute to shared visions, lead instructional change, support policy-making, understand law and ethics, and design high-quality professional learning programs. In addition, they use their technical expertise to select, evaluate, and support the implementation of digital-age teaching, learning, and assessment tools. As technology becomes increasingly enmeshed with mission-critical educational practices, the role of the technology coach will become even more important. Technology coaches already support emerging practices such as data warehousing, online learning, and online testing. The list will continue to grow. Schools need technology coaches in order to realize the full potential of their technology investments.

Educators can use the ISTE Standards • C to garner support for new technology coaches, to defend the importance of existing positions, and to ensure appropriate compensation for highly qualified personnel who can fully implement the standards. While some technology coaches might specialize in a particular performance area, all standards must be implemented to ensure proper support for effective technology implementation. School leaders can use the standards as a list of what needs to occur in the organization and prepare local staffing plans to address them. Without well-prepared, capable educational technology professionals to shape the future of K–12 technology integration, educators cannot meet the learning goals established in national, state, district, and school-level strategic plans.

While the ISTE Standards • C have great potential in helping schools strengthen their technology programs, the work has only just begun. Below are some practical next steps toward fully leveraging their potential:

- Secure necessary translations of the standards to accommodate the language requirements of members of your organization

- Share the standards with stakeholders in order to secure support for technology coaching

- Highlight how the Standards for Coaches support the other ISTE Standards (ISTE

Standards for Students, Teachers, and Administrators) that may be more familiar to stakeholders

- Study/share scenarios in this book as examples of what technology coaches do. Construct your own scenarios to help stakeholders understand what technology coaches do

- Use the standards and/or ISTE's Technology, Coaching, and Community whitepaper to focus technology coaching on new and proven models of personalized, individualized, job-embedded professional learning

- Use the standards to engage leadership and current technology coaches to consider which components of the existing technology coaching program are strong and weak. Design strategies to bridge any gaps.

- Examine existing technology coach-to-teacher ratios and reflect on whether true coaching models are possible based on the number of teachers served.

- Communicate the results of ISTE Standards•C needs assessments to support necessary change

- Use the standards and rubric to examine and improve existing personnel documents such as job postings, job descriptions, interview questions, and performance evaluation guidelines for technology coaches

- Use the standards to recruit and mentor future technology coaches

- Locate and promote professional development and academic degree programs that prepare educators to implement the ISTE Standards•C.

- Use the standards as a self-reflection tool to examine personal technology coaching practices and seek professional learning in areas that would strengthen performance

- Develop communities of practice with other technology coaches, both locally and globally. Share ideas and learn from one another.

Thank you for learning about the ISTE Standards for Coaches and using them to advance effective technology use in your schools and districts. ISTE offers a variety of professional development opportunities at their annual summer conference and online throughout the year. Please share stories of how the standards have helped you and stay involved in future refresh cycles of the standards. Your interest and involvement will insure that the ISTE Standards•C accurately represent the important contributions of technology coaches.

—Jo Williamson

APPENDIX A

ISTE Standards

ISTE Standards for Students (Standards•S)

All K–12 students should be prepared to meet the following standards and performance indicators.

1. CREATIVITY AND INNOVATION

Students demonstrate creative thinking, construct knowledge, and develop innovative products and processes using technology. Students:

a. apply existing knowledge to generate new ideas, products, or processes

b. create original works as a means of personal or group expression

c. use models and simulations to explore complex systems and issues

d. identify trends and forecast possibilities

2. COMMUNICATION AND COLLABORATION

Students use digital media and environments to communicate and work collaboratively, including at a distance, to support individual learning and contribute to the learning of others. Students:

a. interact, collaborate, and publish with peers, experts, or others employing a variety of digital environments and media

b. communicate information and ideas effectively to multiple audiences using a variety of media and formats

c. develop cultural understanding and global awareness by engaging with learners of other cultures

d. contribute to project teams to produce original works or solve problems

3. RESEARCH AND INFORMATION FLUENCY

Students apply digital tools to gather, evaluate, and use information. Students:

a. plan strategies to guide inquiry

b. locate, organize, analyze, evaluate, synthesize, and ethically use information from a variety of sources and media

  c. evaluate and select information sources and digital tools based on the appropriateness to specific tasks

  d. process data and report results

4. CRITICAL THINKING, PROBLEM SOLVING, AND DECISION MAKING

Students use critical-thinking skills to plan and conduct research, manage projects, solve problems, and make informed decisions using appropriate digital tools and resources. Students:

  a. identify and define authentic problems and significant questions for investigation

  b. plan and manage activities to develop a solution or complete a project

  c. collect and analyze data to identify solutions and make informed decisions

  d. use multiple processes and diverse perspectives to explore alternative solutions

5. DIGITAL CITIZENSHIP

Students understand human, cultural, and societal issues related to technology and practice legal and ethical behavior. Students:

  a. advocate and practice the safe, legal, and responsible use of information and technology

  b. exhibit a positive attitude toward using technology that supports collaboration, learning, and productivity

  c. demonstrate personal responsibility for lifelong learning

  d. exhibit leadership for digital citizenship

6. TECHNOLOGY OPERATIONS AND CONCEPTS

Students demonstrate a sound understanding of technology concepts, systems, and operations. Students:

  a. understand and use technology systems

  b. select and use applications effectively and productively

  c. troubleshoot systems and applications

  d. transfer current knowledge to the learning of new technologies

ISTE Standards for Teachers (Standards•T)

All classroom teachers should be prepared to meet the following standards and performance indicators.

1. FACILITATE AND INSPIRE STUDENT LEARNING AND CREATIVITY

Teachers use their knowledge of subject matter, teaching and learning, and technology to facilitate experiences that advance student learning, creativity, and innovation in both face-to-face and virtual environments. Teachers:

a. promote, support, and model creative and innovative thinking and inventiveness

b. engage students in exploring real-world issues and solving authentic problems using digital tools and resources

c. promote student reflection using collaborative tools to reveal and clarify students' conceptual understanding and thinking, planning, and creative processes

d. model collaborative knowledge construction by engaging in learning with students, colleagues, and others in face-to-face and virtual environments

2. DESIGN AND DEVELOP DIGITAL-AGE LEARNING EXPERIENCES AND ASSESSMENTS

Teachers design, develop, and evaluate authentic learning experiences and assessments incorporating contemporary tools and resources to maximize content learning in context and to develop the knowledge, skills, and attitudes identified in the ISTE Standards • S. Teachers:

a. design or adapt relevant learning experiences that incorporate digital tools and resources to promote student learning and creativity

b. develop technology-enriched learning environments that enable all students to pursue their individual curiosities and become active participants in setting their own educational goals, managing their own learning, and assessing their own progress

c. customize and personalize learning activities to address students' diverse learning styles, working strategies, and abilities using digital tools and resources

d. provide students with multiple and varied formative and summative assessments aligned with content and technology standards and use resulting data to inform learning and teaching

3. MODEL DIGITAL-AGE WORK AND LEARNING

Teachers exhibit knowledge, skills, and work processes representative of an innovative professional in a global and digital society. Teachers:

a. demonstrate fluency in technology systems and the transfer of current knowledge to new technologies and situations

b. collaborate with students, peers, parents, and community members using digital tools and resources to support student success and innovation

   c. communicate relevant information and ideas effectively to students, parents, and peers using a variety of digital-age media and formats

   d. model and facilitate effective use of current and emerging digital tools to locate, analyze, evaluate, and use information resources to support research and learning

4. PROMOTE AND MODEL DIGITAL CITIZENSHIP AND RESPONSIBILITY

Teachers understand local and global societal issues and responsibilities in an evolving digital culture and exhibit legal and ethical behavior in their professional practices. Teachers:

   a. advocate, model, and teach safe, legal, and ethical use of digital information and technology, including respect for copyright, intellectual property, and the appropriate documentation of sources

   b. address the diverse needs of all learners by using learner-centered strategies and providing equitable access to appropriate digital tools and resources

   c. promote and model digital etiquette and responsible social interactions related to the use of technology and information

   d. develop and model cultural understanding and global awareness by engaging with colleagues and students of other cultures using digital-age communication and collaboration tools

5. ENGAGE IN PROFESSIONAL GROWTH AND LEADERSHIP

Teachers continuously improve their professional practice, model lifelong learning, and exhibit leadership in their school and professional community by promoting and demonstrating the effective use of digital tools and resources. Teachers:

   a. participate in local and global learning communities to explore creative applications of technology to improve student learning

   b. exhibit leadership by demonstrating a vision of technology infusion, participating in shared decision making and community building, and developing the leadership and technology skills of others

   c. evaluate and reflect on current research and professional practice on a regular basis to make effective use of existing and emerging digital tools and resources in support of student learning

   d. contribute to the effectiveness, vitality, and self-renewal of the teaching profession and of their school and community

ISTE Standards for Administrators (Standards•A)

All school administrators should be prepared to meet the following standards and performance indicators.

1. VISIONARY LEADERSHIP

Educational Administrators inspire and lead development and implementation of a shared vision for comprehensive integration of technology to promote excellence and support transformation throughout the organization.

EDUCATIONAL ADMINISTRATORS:

a. inspire and facilitate among all stakeholders a shared vision of purposeful change that maximizes use of digital-age resources to meet and exceed learning goals, support effective instructional practice, and maximize performance of district and school leaders

b. engage in an ongoing process to develop, implement, and communicate technology-infused strategic plans aligned with a shared vision

c. advocate on local, state, and national levels for policies, programs, and funding to support implementation of a technology-infused vision and strategic plan

2. DIGITAL-AGE LEARNING CULTURE

Educational Administrators create, promote, and sustain a dynamic, digital-age learning culture that provides a rigorous, relevant, and engaging education for all students. Educational Administrators:

a. ensure instructional innovation focused on continuous improvement of digital-age learning

b. model and promote the frequent and effective use of technology for learning

c. provide learner-centered environments equipped with technology and learning resources to meet the individual, diverse needs of all learners

d. ensure effective practice in the study of technology and its infusion across the curriculum

e. promote and participate in local, national, and global learning communities that stimulate innovation, creativity, and digital-age collaboration

3. EXCELLENCE IN PROFESSIONAL PRACTICE

Educational Administrators promote an environment of professional learning and innovation that empowers educators to enhance student learning through the infusion of contemporary technologies and digital resources. Educational Administrators:

a. allocate time, resources, and access to ensure ongoing professional growth in technology fluency and integration

b. facilitate and participate in learning communities that stimulate, nurture, and support administrators, faculty, and staff in the study and use of technology

c. promote and model effective communication and collaboration among stakeholders using digital-age tools

d. stay abreast of educational research and emerging trends regarding effective use of technology and encourage evaluation of new technologies for their potential to improve student learning

4. SYSTEMIC IMPROVEMENT

Educational Administrators provide digital-age leadership and management to continuously improve the organization through the effective use of information and technology resources. Educational Administrators:

a. lead purposeful change to maximize the achievement of learning goals through the appropriate use of technology and media-rich resources

b. collaborate to establish metrics, collect and analyze data, interpret results, and share findings to improve staff performance and student learning

c. recruit and retain highly competent personnel who use technology creatively and proficiently to advance academic and operational goals

d. establish and leverage strategic partnerships to support systemic improvement

e. establish and maintain a robust infrastructure for technology including integrated, interoperable technology systems to support management, operations, teaching, and learning

5. DIGITAL CITIZENSHIP

Educational Administrators model and facilitate understanding of social, ethical, and legal issues and responsibilities related to an evolving digital culture. Educational Administrators:

a. ensure equitable access to appropriate digital tools and resources to meet the needs of all learners

b. promote, model, and establish policies for safe, legal, and ethical use of digital information and technology

c. promote and model responsible social interactions related to the use of technology and information

d. model and facilitate the development of a shared cultural understanding and involvement in global issues through the use of contemporary communication and collaboration tools

ISTE Standards for Coaches (Standards•C)

1. VISIONARY LEADERSHIP

Technology coaches inspire and participate in the development and implementation of a shared vision for the comprehensive integration of technology to promote excellence and support transformational change throughout the instructional environment.

a. Contribute to the development, communication and implementation of a shared vision for the comprehensive use of technology to support a digital age education for all students.

b. Contribute to the planning, development, communication, implementation and evaluation of technology-infused strategic plans at the district and school levels.

c. Advocate for policies, procedures, programs and funding strategies to support implementation of the shared vision represented in the school and district technology plans and guidelines.

d. Implement strategies for initiating and sustaining technology innovations and manage the change process in schools and classrooms.

2. TEACHING, LEARNING AND ASSESSMENTS

Technology coaches assist teachers in using technology effectively for assessing student learning, differentiating instruction and providing rigorous, relevant and engaging learning experiences for all students.

a. Coach teachers in and model design and implementation of technology-enhanced learning experiences addressing content standards and student technology standards.

b. Coach teachers in and model design and implementation of technology-enhanced learning experiences using a variety of research-based, learner-centered instructional strategies and assessment tools to address the diverse needs and interests of all students.

c. Coach teachers in and model engagement of students in local and global inter-disciplinary units in which technology helps students assume professional roles, research real-world problems, collaborate with others and produce products that are meaningful and useful to a wide audience.

d. Coach teachers in and model design and implementation of technology-enhanced learning experiences emphasizing creativity, higher-order thinking skills and processes and mental habits of mind (e.g., critical thinking, meta-cognition and self-regulation).

e. Coach teachers in and model design and implementation of technology-enhanced learning experiences using differentiation, including adjusting content, process, product and learning environment based upon student readiness levels, learning styles, interests and personal goals.

f. Coach teachers in and model incorporation of research-based best practices in instructional design when planning technology-enhanced learning experiences.

g. Coach teachers in and model effective use of technology tools and resources to continuously assess student learning and technology literacy by applying a rich variety of formative and summative assessments aligned with content and student technology standards.

h. Coach teachers in and model effective use of technology tools and resources to systematically collect and analyze student achievement data, interpret results and communicate findings to improve instructional practice and maximize student learning.

3. DIGITAL AGE LEARNING ENVIRONMENTS

Technology coaches create and support effective digital age learning environments to maximize the learning of all students.

a. Model effective classroom management and collaborative learning strategies to maximize teacher and student use of digital tools and resources and access to technology-rich learning environments.

b. Maintain and manage a variety of digital tools and resources for teacher and student use in technology-rich learning environments.

c. Coach teachers in and model use of online and blended learning, digital content and collaborative learning networks to support and extend student learning as well as expand opportunities and choices for online professional development for teachers and administrators.

d. Select, evaluate and facilitate the use of adaptive and assistive technologies to support student learning.

e. Troubleshoot basic software, hardware and connectivity problems common in digital learning environments.

f. Collaborate with teachers and administrators to select and evaluate digital tools and resources that enhance teaching and learning and are compatible with the school technology infrastructure.

g. Use digital communication and collaboration tools to communicate locally and globally with students, parents, peers and the larger community.

4. PROFESSIONAL DEVELOPMENT AND PROGRAM EVALUATION

Technology coaches conduct needs assessments, develop technology-related professional learning programs and evaluate the impact on instructional practice and student learning.

a. Conduct needs assessments to inform the content and delivery of technology-related professional learning programs that result in a positive impact on student learning.

b. Design, develop and implement technology-rich professional learning programs that model principles of adult learning and promote digital age best practices in teaching, learning and assessment.

c. Evaluate results of professional learning programs to determine the effectiveness on deepening teacher content knowledge, improving teacher pedagogical skills and/or increasing student learning.

5. DIGITAL CITIZENSHIP

Technology coaches model and promote digital citizenship.

a. Model and promote strategies for achieving equitable access to digital tools and resources and technology-related best practices for all students and teachers.

b. Model and facilitate safe, healthy, legal and ethical uses of digital information and technologies.

c. Model and promote diversity, cultural understanding and global awareness by using digital age communication and collaboration tools to interact locally and globally with students, peers, parents and the larger community.

6. CONTENT KNOWLEDGE AND PROFESSIONAL GROWTH

Technology coaches demonstrate professional knowledge, skills and dispositions in content, pedagogical and technological areas as well as adult learning and leadership and are continuously deepening their knowledge and expertise.

a. Engage in continual learning to deepen content and pedagogical knowledge in technology integration and current and emerging technologies necessary to effectively implement the ISTE Standards•S and ISTE Standards•T.

b. Engage in continuous learning to deepen professional knowledge, skills and dispositions in organizational change and leadership, project management and adult learning to improve professional practice.

c. Regularly evaluate and reflect on their professional practice and dispositions to improve and strengthen their ability to effectively model and facilitate technology-enhanced learning experiences.

ISTE Standards for Computer Science Educators (Standards•CSE)

1. KNOWLEDGE OF CONTENT

Computer Science Educators demonstrate knowledge of Computer Science content and model important principles and concepts.

a. Demonstrate knowledge of and proficiency in data representation and abstraction

i. Effectively use primitive data types

ii. Demonstrate an understanding of static and dynamic data structures

iii. Effectively use, manipulate, and explain various external data stores: various types (text, images, sound, etc.), various locations (local, server, cloud), etc.

iv. Effectively use modeling and simulation to solve real-world problems

b. **Effectively design, develop, and test algorithms**

   i. Using a modern, high-level programming language, construct correctly functioning programs involving simple and structured data types; compound boolean expressions; and sequential, conditional, and iterative control structures

   ii. Design and test algorithms and programming solutions to problems in different contexts (textual, numeric, graphic, etc.) using advanced data structures

   iii. Analyze algorithms by considering complexity, efficiency, aesthetics, and correctness

   iv. Demonstrate knowledge of two or more programming paradigms

   v. Effectively use two or more development environments

   vi. Demonstrate knowledge of varied software development models and project management strategies

c. **Demonstrate knowledge of digital devices, systems, and networks**

   i. Demonstrate an understanding of data representation at the machine level

   ii. Demonstrate an understanding of machine- level components and related issues of complexity

   iii. Demonstrate an understanding of operating systems and networking in a structured computer system

   iv. Demonstrate an understanding of the operation of computer networks and mobile computing devices

d. **Demonstrate an understanding of the role computer science plays and its impact in the modern world**

   i. Demonstrate an understanding of the social, ethical, and legal issues and impacts of computing, and attendant responsibilities of computer scientists and users

   ii. Analyze the contributions of computer science to current and future innovations in sciences, humanities, the arts, and commerce

2. EFFECTIVE TEACHING AND LEARNING STRATEGIES

Computer Science Educators demonstrate effective content pedagogical strategies that make the discipline comprehensible to students.

a. **Plan and teach computer science lessons/units using effective and engaging practices and methodologies**

   i. Select a variety of real-world computing problems and project-based methodologies that support active and authentic learning and provide opportunities for creative and innovative thinking and problem solving

   ii. Demonstrate the use of a variety of collaborative groupings in lesson plans/ units and assessments

iii. Design activities that require students to effectively describe computing artifacts and communicate results using multiple forms of media

iv. Develop lessons and methods that engage and empower learners from diverse cultural and linguistic backgrounds

v. Identify problematic concepts and constructs in computer science and appropriate strategies to address them

vi. Design and implement developmentally appropriate learning opportunities supporting the diverse needs of all learners

vii.Create and implement multiple forms of assessment and use resulting data to capture student learning, provide remediation, and shape classroom instruction

3. EFFECTIVE LEARNING ENVIRONMENTS

Computer Science Educators apply their knowledge of learning environments by creating and maintaining safe, ethical, supportive, fair, and effective learning environments for all students.

a. **Design environments that promote effective teaching and learning in computer science classrooms and online learning environments and promote digital citizenship**

i. Promote and model the safe and effective use of computer hardware, software, peripherals, and networks

ii. Plan for equitable and accessible classroom, lab, and online environments that support effective and engaging learning

4. EFFECTIVE PROFESSIONAL KNOWLEDGE AND SKILLS

Computer Science Educators demonstrate professional knowledge and skills in their field and readiness to apply them.

a. **Participate in, promote, and model ongoing professional development and life-long learning relative to computer science and computer science education**

i. Identify and participate in professional computer science and computer science education societies, organizations, and groups that provide professional growth opportunities and resources

ii. Demonstrate knowledge of evolving social and research issues relating to computer science and computer science education

iii. Identify local, state, and national content and professional standards and requirements affecting the teaching of secondary computer science

Standards•CSE © 2011 International Society for Technology in Education.

APPENDIX B

Alignment between ISTE Essential Conditions and ISTE Standards for Technology Coaches (ISTE Standards•C)

This chart illustrates how ISTE Essential Conditions are aligned with ISTE Standards•C.

	ISTE Standards•C					
ESSENTIAL CONDITIONS	1. VISIONARY LEADERSHIP	2. TEACHING, LEARNING, & ASSESSMENT	3. DIGITAL AGE LEARNING ENVIRONMENTS	4. PROFESSIONAL DEVELOPMENT & PROGRAM EVALUATION	5. DIGITAL CITIZENSHIP	6. CONTENT KNOWLEDGE & PROFESSIONAL GROWTH
Shared Vision						
Proactive leadership develops a shared vision for educational technology among all education stakeholders, including teachers and support staff, school and district administrators, teacher educators, students, parents, and the community.	●					
Empowered Leaders						
Stakeholders at every level are empowered to be leaders in effecting change	●					

	ISTE Standards•C					
ESSENTIAL CONDITIONS	1. VISIONARY LEADERSHIP	2. TEACHING, LEARNING, & ASSESSMENT	3. DIGITAL AGE LEARNING ENVIRONMENTS	4. PROFESSIONAL DEVELOPMENT & PROGRAM EVALUATION	5. DIGITAL CITIZENSHIP	6. CONTENT KNOWLEDGE & PROFESSIONAL GROWTH
Implementation Planning All stakeholders follow a systematic plan aligned with a shared vision for school effectiveness and student learning through the infusion of information and communication technology (ICT) and digital learning resources.	●					
Consistent and Adequate Funding Ongoing funding supports technology infrastructure, personnel, digital resources, and staff development.	●					
Equitable Access All students, teachers, staff, and school leaders have robust and reliable connectivity and access to current and emerging technologies and digital resources.					●	
Skilled Personnel Educators, support staff, and other leaders are skilled in the selection and effective use of appropriate ICT resources.				●		●

ESSENTIAL CONDITIONS	1. VISIONARY LEADERSHIP	2. TEACHING, LEARNING, & ASSESSMENT	3. DIGITAL AGE LEARNING ENVIRON-MENTS	4. PROFESSIONAL DEVELOP-MENT & PROGRAM EVALUATION	5. DIGITAL CITIZEN-SHIP	6. CONTENT KNOWLEDGE & PROFES-SIONAL GROWTH
Ongoing Professional Learning — Educators have ongoing access to technology-related professional learning plans and opportunities as well as dedicated time to practice and share ideas.				●		●
Technical Support — Educators and students have access to reliable assistance for maintaining, renewing, and using ICT and digital learning resources.			●			
Curriculum Framework — Content standards and related digital curriculum resources align with and support digital age learning and work.		●	●			
Student-Centered Learning — Planning, teaching, and assessment all center on the needs and abilities of the students.		●				

ISTE Standards•C						
ESSENTIAL CONDITIONS	1. VISIONARY LEADERSHIP	2. TEACHING, LEARNING, & ASSESSMENT	3. DIGITAL AGE LEARNING ENVIRONMENTS	4. PROFESSIONAL DEVELOPMENT & PROGRAM EVALUATION	5. DIGITAL CITIZENSHIP	6. CONTENT KNOWLEDGE & PROFESSIONAL GROWTH
Assessment and Evaluation Teaching, learning, leadership, and the use of ICT and digital resources are continually assessed and evaluated.		●		●		
Engaged Communities Leaders and educators develop and maintain partnerships and collaboration within the community to support and fund the use of ICT and digital learning resources	●				●	
Support Policies Policies, financial plans, accountability measures, and incentive structures support the use of ICT and other digital resources for both learning and district/school operations	●				●	
Supportive External Context Policies and initiatives at the national, regional, and local levels support schools and teacher preparation programs in the effective implementation of technology for achieving curriculum and learning technology standards.	●				●	

Sources: www.iste.org/standards/essential-conditions; www.iste.org/standards/iste-standards/standards-for-coaches